THE COMMAND
OF MELCHIZEDEK

Published by Revival Waves of Glory Books & Publishing

PO Box 596| Litchfield, Illinois 62056 USA

www.revivalwavesofgloryministries.com

Revival Waves of Glory Books & Publishing is committed to excellence in the publishing industry.

Book design Copyright © 2017 by Revival Waves of Glory Books & Publishing. All rights reserved.

Published in the United States of America

Paperback: 978-1-365-87407-9

THE
COMMAND
OF
MELCHIZEDEK

"Let all the angels of God, worship HIM."

DANIEL OYEGUN

Table of Contents

Dedication

To the invisible, immortal priest of God the Father, Melchizedek; the eternal God who is without father or mother, without beginning of days nor end of life, and who, like the Son of God Jesus, remains a priest forever in heaven, your eternal command stands sure forever with these words, "Let ALL the angels of God, worship him."

Appreciation

Abig thank you to my wife, Claribelle Baccay-Oyegun, without whom this work would never have seen the light of day; you are a beacon of light and hope to me, your endless encouragement gave me the valour needed to put this work in print as a testimony to the word of God.

To Pastor Chris Oyakhilome of Christ Embassy, Inc.; as an expert craftsman, you laid the word foundation on which I now build. I was born again through the word of God spoken by you and I am blessed to have had my first spiritual word nourishing under your ministry. I say a big thank you for you have been an inspiration in my life. May the Lord continually spread you, Amen.

To Pastor Paul Adefarasin of House on the Rock, Inc.; the word of Hope you preach instilled in me a doggedness which prepared me for the test and I am grateful for I passed that test, but without you I could not, for you a blessing to my generation. May the Lord continually increase you, Amen.

And finally, to the Bishop of Bishops, Bishop David Oyedepo of Living Faith Church, Inc., aka Winners Chapel; the word of Faith you teach gave me the discipline I needed to rise up after my test and fulfil the word of God for a testimony to this generation. I say a big thank you, sir.

Introduction

The degree to which we communicate spiritual truth depends on the degree to which we understand them and the elect are those of their own will who choose to be instruments of God's will in accordance with divine purpose and plan. These are keepers of the prophecies of Elohim, bearers of light and the message of truth which prophecies are the means to convey and preserve the will and power of God not only in the lives of men but also here on the earth and through men there in heaven.

To properly understand and interpret the books of scripture, we must first understand what was in the mind of the author at the time those words were being written. To fall short of this is to create conjectures of self-assimilation and comprehension. This breeds the numerous doctrines and religious dogma that abound because there is no clear cut understanding of the author's very thoughts when he penned his words. This is no ordinary book, this is a spiritual book and it's light is the light of the word of God, hence, it is for the chosen amongst the called, the select amongst the elect, and it is for those who seek not only a deeper knowledge of the Bible but also an ever increasing conscious awareness of the invisible presence of the ghost from heaven, even, the Holy Ghost.

Jesus Christ in his present form is an unseen reality and man has the capacity to make God real to him and a reality in existence or to make God a non-entity whose very existence is not only questionable but in itself non-existent. All this is subject to man's choosing to acknowledge consciously the reality of the invisible and the paranormal activity which follows such conscious belief. A time will come and is come when men will stagger from coast to coast in search for the Word of the Lord and many will not find it for there will be a dearth of God's word. But the earth shall be filled with the true knowledge of the glory of God in Christ Jesus and I will not be counted as one of those who held the knowledge of God in unrighteousness for that which may be known of God has been made known to me and I will let it be known. The Apostle Paul preached Christ crucified, that was his theology, and we teach Christ, heaven's high priest in the order of Melchizedek and contrary to popular opinion, the book of Hebrews was not written to Jewish believers; it was written to all who believe in Jesus that we may know Jesus now serves as high priest in heaven, in the order of God's priest, Melchizedek.

The greatest demand of God is to live by faith. And as simple as it reads, it requires much more than just believing the written word. For to live by faith is to live by and pattern your very life in accordance with every word of God that comes to you whether it negates common sense or it makes sense to you or others, for most times

God demands of us the incredulous and that which we normally would not do and when you get to this point, then you know you're living by the very word of God. With neither predecessor nor precedence other than the words written in the books of God's word, we make a defense every day for the gospel we teach, so like the Apostle Paul, I say, according to the gospel given to me from above, through the prophetic scriptures of God's word, Jesus is a priest in heaven, after the command and order of the God and priest Melchizedek, who is the eternal, immortal priest of the Father, the Most-high God. Man condemns what he understands not while striving for what is not. We are taking men from the seen realm to the unseen realm, introducing them from the known to the unknown. Erase your doubts and let faith fill your heart to overflow.

In my first book, *The Person of Melchizedek*, reluctantly I engaged myself in putting down my thoughts as the spirit led me. Having no precedence to refer to, I wrote as one reluctantly discharging a service handed down. I have tried to run away from these words, as they seemed to overcome my very own thought processes, however, one can only run so far when God insists on you, hence, it dawns on me the very purpose for which I was created, and with this work, we shall give light to the chosen and to whom are called by the eternal king and the eternal priest. The observable effects of God's word leave me beyond doubt but to accept and embrace that which is my call that we may answer as I now have and open the understanding of the many to whom we are sent. Once I understood what the Apostle Paul meant when he called the word of God a sacred secret, I stopped trying to convince people to believe the word of faith we speak for these words are hidden and can only be understood when revealed by the Spirit of God, and even though men read the words or hear them spoken, it would only be plain words, just as the Bible is to the many today. But as I found out from the "Year of the Double Portion", whoever gains the word of these thoughts, gains a power hitherto unknown to them. We have much to say but you cannot bear them now for we want the reader to understand our words thought for thought and not just word for word. However, as new wineskins are prepared for the new wine brewed and ready to be poured, I pray your spirit is set right that you may apprehend truth in its purest form, to see that truth, which is revealed in us, that it might be in you. To share divine truth from the very depths of God's word, we know who, what and in whom we are; that great eternal ghost, invisible in presence and spiritual in essence we come alive to, that we may feed our souls in the essence of his truth. There are new wineskins for new wine. The message is new wine, and we are the new wineskins. This is the command as I was told it and this is the order of Melchizedek.

"I have spoken of earthly things and you do not believe, how then can you believe if I tell you of heavenly things?" - Jesus

Chapter One

Beresiyt Bara Elohim

"In the beginning, Gods created the heavens and the earth..." Genesis 1:1

I t all began May 1st, 2001, barely over a week since he got born again on April 22 of the same year. On a fateful Tuesday evening, sitting outside the hostel where he lodged at school, with everyone one else indoors, thinking to himself all alone, lost in deep thoughts about who God really is, when suddenly he heard a voice speak, saying, *"Look up into the sky."* In response he says to himself, "Look into the sky for what?" The voice came again, with a strong intonation, *"I said, look up into the sky, search... you will see my face."* Slowly, he lifts his head up looking up to the sky and wondering if he was sane, when all of a sudden the cumulus clouds above began taking on the shape of a man's face. Alarmed, he starts to get up, intending to run indoors and call out the others to see what he was seeing, when the voice spoke again, *"Sit down; they will think you are crazy."* Slowly, and unable to resist the command, he sits down staring into the face that had been formed by the clouds. Then the words came, *"You will know me, you will know me beyond the extreme, you will live my life beyond the extreme for I have chosen to show my holiness through you, to show myself strong on behalf of my saints through you to the praise of my glory. You will live beyond the extreme I promise you, beyond the extreme."* These were the words spoken on that fateful day and slowly cirrus clouds began to blow over the face formed by cumulus until it was all gone. I know the day for I wrote the very words down myself and I still have my Journal from 2003 when I transcribed the words spoken. I recall speaking with a flat mate, Dennis *(real name),* the following day about the experience and he laughed at me saying, *"You mean you saw God's face in the clouds?"* In retrospect, I can understand the sarcastic tone in his voice and it all makes sense now. This was the Genesis of all things written herein, the start of his journey into things unseen.

In my previous book, *The Person of Melchizedek,* I explained the identity of Melchizedek but I will here restate from *The Person of Melchizedek* on the personality of God's very own priest.

Much has been said about the person and order of Melchizedek in whose priesthood Jesus is revealed to be in as it is written in the scriptures. Some have taught and still teach the visitation to Abraham in the Old Testament as a manifestation of the pre-incarnate Christ, others supposing Him to be a Canaanite priest-king, still others an angel of God or the Holy Spirit. But many a times we have failed to question our beliefs not for the purpose of being critical but for the knowledge we would be afforded if only we could just lay hold on the truth.

The accounts we have of Melchizedek are found in Gen 14:18-20 and in Psalm 110:4. But the book of Hebrews chapter 7:1-8 gives us a rather detailed description of his

2

person. These verses of scripture are by far the most intriguing in the New Testament. Born of the revelation of God's Spirit to the apostle, their central theme is the expression of the person of Melchizedek, communicating sacred truth of the mysteries of God as expressed in the Old Testament which before then was unknown to the church until at God's appointed time by His Spirit it was revealed through His word to the apostle.

In writing the epistle to the Hebrews about the priest, Melchizedek, the apostle says, "*Of whom we have many things to say and hard to be uttered.*"

Of Melchizedek, we begin with the question that first offers itself; who is Melchizedek, the priest of the Most-high God? In order to better aid our understanding, we shall here give a thought for thought comparative paraphrase of Hebrews chapter 7 vs. 1-8. Let's understand that this paraphrase and its meaning is not another interpretation of these verses but exclusively for the purpose of conveying the interpretation of it as was intended by the apostle to the recipients of the Epistle and they serve only to aid our understanding of these inspired verses of scripture, giving us an insight into the mind of Christ as revealed by the Spirit of God to the apostle.

Hebrews, Chapter 7:1-3 KJV: *1For this Melchizedek, king of Salem, priest of the Most-high God, who met Abraham returning from the slaughter of the kings, and blessed him; 2To whom also Abraham gave a tenth part of all; first being by interpretation King of Righteousness, and after that also King of Salem, which is King of peace; 3Without father, without mother, without descent, having neither beginning of days nor end of life; but made like unto the Son of God; abideth a priest continually.*

Paraphrase verses 1-3: **1***For this Melchizedek, [whose name means] king of Salem, [is the Immortal] priest of the Most-high God [in heaven], He met with Abraham as he returned from the defeat of the kings and blessed him;* **2***To whom also Abraham gave a tenth part of all; first being by interpretation [His name Melchizedek means] king of righteousness, and after that, [as said before it] also [means] King of Salem, which is King of peace;* **3***Without father, without mother, without descent, [indeed without origin, He is Immortal Spirit, a celestial being] having neither beginning of days nor end of life; but made like the Son of God; [he remains] a priest forever.*

First, we understand Melchizedek was never at any given time king of any city called Salem, the language of verse two gives us to know that king of Salem is another meaning to his name, it says first being translated, because there is a second meaning to his name. In writing the Epistle to the Hebrews, the apostle reveals Melchizedek to be the immortal priest of God in heaven, one who has lived with the Father from the beginning of time till date and who will remain His priest forever.

He declares Melchizedek to be without origin, having neither beginning of days nor end of life. Indeed Melchizedek was not created and is the head of the order of "Melchizedek", the royal order and priesthood to which even our Lord Jesus belongs and to which we all in Christ also belong. In Genesis, Melchizedek appeared as a man, a stranger to Abraham, and gave him bread and wine and received the tithe from Abraham. We shouldn't be surprised at this for scripture teaches us that even in these times, spirits still appear as strangers to many. The reason Moses being on Mount Sinai was given to know the meaning of the name is because it is not an earthly name and as such men would never have been able to comprehend its meaning. Melchizedek bears both names for from the Father the whole family in heaven and on earth derives its name. The name of every member of the household of God must attest to His (God's) greatness.

The order of Aaron, which was introduced at Mount Sinai, was only a copy of the order of Melchizedek in heaven and it was to serve until the coming of the Christ who would redeem man from sin and who would show him the way of truth, giving him access into the very presence of God.

The law and all its ordinances were only a shadow of the true things, the reality and fulfillment however is found in Christ and as it is declared of him in the scriptures, Jesus today in heaven is "*a priest forever after the order of Melchizedek.*" The reason being that there in heaven long before any angel, cherub or seraph was created, Melchizedek is and when this earth would be no more, Melchizedek will still be the eternal immortal priest of the Most-high God, a minister of the true sanctuary set up by the Lord himself.

Of the altar whereof Melchizedek is priest in the presence of God, the scriptures spectacularly reveal in Revelation 8:3-4. "*And another angel came and stood at the altar, having a golden censer, and there was given unto him much incense, that he should offer it with the prayers of all saints upon the golden altar which was before the throne.*

And the smoke of the incense, which came with the prayers of the saints, ascended up before God out of the angel's hand. (Emphasis added)

Here, we are given to know amongst other things in heaven the temple ordinances Melchizedek presides over in the presence of God and also to know this day that incense is offered onto God in heaven as the Levites did back then on earth in the dispensation of the Aaronic Priesthood, such that at the time the earthly tabernacle was still standing in Israel and the priests burnt incense onto God, there in Zion the city of the living God, angels were also offering incense to him as they do to this day even as you read this book.

And to this day, Melchizedek is the priest overseeing the activities at this altar as it's always been part of the duties as priest of God Most-high. If Melchizedek is not Gods priest in Zion, then Jesus in Zion is not high priest in the order of Melchizedek. But as it is written, Melchizedek is the priest of God Most-high and Jesus is a priest forever in the order of Melchizedek, Gods own priest. We must understand that whenever the scripture refers to Jesus as high priest, it's not an exaltation of his person but the reality of truth as sure as there is no other name given under heaven by God through which we can be saved other than the name and person of Jesus.

Concerning this great immortal priest of God, the word goes on to say in Hebrews 7:4-6 KJV: *⁴Now consider how great this man was, unto whom even the patriarch Abraham gave the tenth of the spoils. ⁵And verily they that are of the sons of Levi, who receive the office of the priesthood, have a commandment to take tithes of the people according to the law, that is, of their brethren, though they come out of the loins of Abraham. 6But he whose descent is not counted from them received tithes of Abraham, and blessed him that had the promises.*

Paraphrase verses 4-6: *4Now consider how great this [one is], unto whom even the patriarch Abraham gave the tenth of the spoils.5And verily they that are of the sons of Levi, who receive the office of the priesthood, have a commandment to take tithes of the people according to the law, that is, of their brethren, though they come out of the loins of Abraham. 6But he whose descent is not counted from them received tithes of Abraham, and blessed him that had the promises.*

According to the New Testament in original Greek, the word translated man in verse 4 by the scholars of the Authorized Version originally read to imply "one" and as such they grossly translated it to mean man thereby taking the accuracy of its understanding out of place and making this chapter of the entire scripture confusing and difficult to comprehend. And all over the scriptures, we find several instances where angels are referred to as men, such as Daniel referred to the angel Gabriel as a man.

The apostle here sets out to convince the Hebrew Christians and the rest of us of the greatness of Melchizedek such that at the time he came to the earth and met with Abraham; he not only received tithes of him but also blessed Abraham who in the sight of **God** is the father of us all. It is well known that the greater person gives his blessing to the lesser one and the spiritual importance of this historic meeting will forever be felt.

KJV verses 7-8; *7And without all contradiction the less is blessed of the better.*

8And here men that die receive tithes; but there he receiveth them, of whom it is witnessed that he liveth.

Paraphrase verses 7-8; *7And without all contradiction the less is blessed of the better. 8And here [in this world] men that die receive tithes; but there [in the city of God] he receives them [the tithes], he [Melchizedek] of whom it is witnessed that he lives forever.*

As part of Melchizedek's responsibility in the city of Zion, the apostle in verse 8 says there in the city of God, Melchizedek receives the tithe. We must understand the Jews were asked to pay tithe to the high priests of the Levitical Priesthood who were descendants of Aaron for it was a copy of what avails in the city of God though the order of Aaron was founded on an earthly order based on a carnal commandment. The law and all its regulations that came with it including tithing were only a copy of the real things and as a copy of the order of Melchizedek they [the priests] were by the law empowered to receive tithes according to the priesthood to which they belonged.

Melchizedek: A True Deity

The apostle reveals Melchizedek as having no beginning to his days or end to his life, thus ascribing immortality to Melchizedek, which undoubtedly in all of scripture is witnessed also of God the Father as being immortal and incorruptible. Melchizedek alone, other than Jesus, is revealed to have been with God from eternity and will yet remain forever. In both the Old and New

Testaments, God is repeatedly ascribed the title "the Most-high God". I believe it is so because there are other "gods" that he is higher than in authority, more so as the scriptures affirm him to be a reigning king with Melchizedek as his priest, while also having twenty-four elders (Rev. 4:4) about whom we are told nothing whether they be created or not. But knowing the things revealed belong to us and our children while the secret things belong to God (Deuteronomy 29:29), we will be none the wiser to assume he is the Most-high God over himself if not these, as Jesus shares his same authority being beside him. The apostle affirms Melchizedek is *without father or mother or descent; having neither beginning of days nor end of life,* and *he abideth forever."* (Hebrews 7:3). In light of these attributes, which I consider, necessary as constituting a true deity, Melchizedek in scripture is acclaimed a God in heaven, one of the *Elohim* and priest of the Most-high God.

The first book (Genesis) of the Torah, in the very words of Moses, begins with these words, "Beresiyt Bara Elohim", meaning, "In the beginning, Gods'..." The Hebrew Torah uses the word Elohim, which is the Hebrew plural verb meaning Gods, the singular verb translated in the King James Version reads, El or Eloah, which would translate Genesis 1:1 to mean, "In the beginning, God..." This is what we have in today's translations, but to properly comprehend the Bible, the need arises for us to read in light of the original tongues. Many have said this indicates no plurality in the Godhead, but this is a lie of the devil for God speaks with intent, and if Moses says Gods, he means just that, **Gods**. Thus, Moses introduces Elohim to us, apparent with the fact that the Holy books begin with the words, "In the beginning, GODS created the heavens and the earth.

There has always been two Gods from the beginning of time till date; the king who is the father, and Melchizedek, his priest. Together, they form the Godhead. The Godhead is made up of these two and together the Godhead is referred to as one authority, that is, when they act together, they are referred to as one. In reality though, it is actually the God-king and the God-priest. This is the Godhead. The Godhead is one authority, though made up of two persons, which is why Jesus today is one person but possesses the power of these two Gods, as Jesus is the fullness of the Godhead and we are complete in Him (Colossians 2:9), having the authority of the king and the authority of the priest.

In the Old Testament, we find the word Elohim, which is a plural verb in many portions of the Bible. Whenever we find this verb in place, it refers to the King and his priest, and the word **Elohim** means *Gods*. The God-head is one entity made up of two persons, the Father, who is king, and Melchizedek, who is his priest. Melchizedek is the Father's Priest while the Father is Melchizedek's King. I speak about the God who is priest in heaven, the God who was before the beginning, the one who stood by the Father when he said; "Let us make man". The God after whose order and command Jesus is a priest in heaven. Melchizedek is the name of the priest of God the Father, one who is without beginning of days or end of life, one who is immortal and incorruptible and one who lives forever.

Chapter Two

The Command of Melchizedek

"And when he bringeth in the first begotten into the world, he saith, 'Let all the angels of God worship Him.'"
(Hebrews 1:6)

J anuary 2004, in *"The Year of the Double Portion"*, as Pastor Chris of Christ Embassy Church aka Believer's Loveworld dubbed it, somewhere in the first month, a vision of the night beckons, while men were fast asleep, the word of the Lord was secretly brought in. Walking on a road less travelled, there stood a man and his wife holding open the Bible, both ministers of the gospel, keepers of God's word, and as he passed by, she motioned with a wave. When he comes to them, the wife, being the one who spoke said, *"Brother please explain this portion of the Bible to us because we don't understand it."* (They were reading from the book of Hebrews) Taking the Bible from them, he begins to expound the scriptures. Having done that, he made to close the book, and suddenly the Bible had changed to a book written by him, with a picture on the back cover of one dressed in the full armor of God, a picture of him walking on a large cobbled road, with an expanded building to his left representing the United States, and two other smaller buildings to his right, the first seemingly Great Britain, followed by France next to it, and underneath where the words written, *"He is called an apostle of God, with the gift of stirring up the nations in the things that pertain to God."* Upon reading, he awoke.

"However, it is not possible for men to avoid fate, although they see it beforehand." - Flavius Josephus

In reading the book of Hebrews, many a time we fail to realize the book does not begin with earthly events, it chronicles and begins with events which took place in heaven after the resurrection, for it says, "...when he had by himself purged our sins, he sat down at the right hand of the Majesty on high." (Hebrews 1:3b) Further down in verse 6, it states, "And again, when he bringeth in the first begotten into the world..." Let's understand the world referred here is not the world of men, it is heaven, the parallel world which exists with the earth, it is the world where God lives, for just before, we are told Jesus sat down at the right hand of the Majesty on high. And again, Jesus only became the first begotten after his resurrection, while in the flesh he was the only begotten of the Father, full of grace and truth.

The Greek word translated as "order" is the word taxis, which means command, rank, file, etc. In writing the epistle to the Hebrews, the apostle repeats the words of the psalmist, "You are a priest forever after the order (command, rank, file, etc.) of Melchizedek." The apostle not only makes a proper case in demonstrating the superiority of Jesus over the angels, he lets us know the events which took place in heaven after the resurrection of Jesus and the subsequent heavenly declaration which was decreed in heaven. Let us here examine the verses below.

⁵ For unto which of the angels said he at any time, "Thou art my Son, this day have I begotten thee?" And again, "I will be to him a Father, and he shall be to me a Son? ⁶ And again, when he bringeth in the first begotten into the world, he saith; "Let all the angels of God worship him."

First, the Apostle gives us to know that after Jesus' resurrection, the Father said to him in heaven, "You are my son; today I have become your father." This was in the presence of the twenty four elders, the general assembly, the holy angels, the spirits of just men made perfect and his priest, Melchizedek. The apostle further states the father also said, "I will be a father to him and he will be my son. Obviously, this statement is to those present there in heaven and not directed to the son himself, but the apostle reveals to us a remarkable heavenly proclamation, he further says, "And again, when he bringeth in the first begotten into the world, he saith, '**Let all the angels of God worship him.'**"

This is the order of Melchizedek, "Let all the angels of God worship him..." It is the command of Melchizedek, the apostle gives us to know that after the resurrection of Jesus, in the presence of all in heaven, a command, an order, an edict was issued and decreed in heaven, it was and still is in effect, a heavenly proclamation to every angel (messenger, servant, spirits and men alike) to worship Jesus. We know Melchizedek gave the order, for it says, "Let all the angels of GOD, worship him." Obviously, from the verse, it is clear the Father himself did not speak these words, for the words, "of God", indicate the above words were spoken by someone other than the Father who is king and God over all. "Let all the angels of God worship him." The Father definitely is not talking and referring to himself as God? Someone else did. God himself said to Jesus, "You are a priest forever after the order of Melchizedek." This was spoken by the king and with an oath. Any decision taken is subject to agreement between the two parties of the Godhead, that's why Genesis 1:26 says, "Let us..." The king didn't say, 'Let me', he said, 'Let us.' He is the Most-high God because; there is another God he is higher than. And the word let means allow. Let us means allow us. This is the command of Melchizedek and this brings us the role of the priest in heaven.

Melchizedek as a God and Priest is the administrator of the Father's word, the keeper and enforcer of the king's word. The Old Testament is replete with many indications of the priest functioning in this role and this was regarding the earthly priest who served as a shadow of the true temple in heaven. Melchizedek is the person who decrees the words of the Father and they become law which is why she decreed the above order, the reason why at the mention of the name of Jesus, every knee should bow, in heaven, on earth and under the earth, why? For the word of the priest is the law of God.

Where there is a change in the priesthood, there is necessarily a change of the law also (Hebrews 7:11) even in heaven. Since there was a change in the position of priest, from Melchizedek to Jesus, a new command, a new order and decree had to be promulgated. The office of high priest shifted from Melchizedek to Jesus, hence the reason the order of Melchizedek saying, "Let all the angels of God worship him." All other laws in heaven are summed up in

14

this one law thus making the words of Jesus law. The message we bring has in it amongst others, the power to stir you up in the things that pertain to God, the power to save and the power to command the spirits so that they obey you, indeed, it is the order of Melchizedek we live by, for it says thus, "Let all the angels of God, worship Him..." (Hebrews 1:6) This is the command of Melchizedek, now you know why the name of Jesus has power for the command has gone forth from the priest of the Most-high God in heaven.

Hebrews 1:6 lets us know that when Jesus was made a priest and presented before the general assembly in heaven, the order of Melchizedek went thus, "Let all the angels of God worship him." We know the command of Melchizedek and when Melchizedek says all, meaning all, from the twenty-four elder gods, to Michael, Gabriel, even Lucifer, etc. This is the order of Melchizedek and we partake of that command for we are joint heirs with Jesus and what was said to one was said to all. Let all the angels of God, worship Jesus, and all of men who believe in him. This is the authority of a believer, this is the order of Melchizedek, "Let all the angels of God, worship him!"

Someone once asked me, of what use is the knowledge of the person of Melchizedek? My response was simply this, "In the beginning, Gods created the heavens and the earth." Why would anyone want the word "Gods" supplanted with "God"? The answer is simple; to hide a truth, to suppress it in its fullness so man would not attain a certain level of deliverance spiritually. "For through knowledge shall the just be delivered." What truth one may ask? The truth that if Melchizedek as God's priest is relatively unheard of as a God, then the command of Melchizedek in Hebrews 1:6 is of no effect, which command states, "Let ALL the ANGELS of God worship Him." Worship who? Worship Jesus and the man in Christ. ANGELS are to Worship YOU, it is the command of God.

Moses writes **Gods** but men changed it to **God**. But the alterations don't affect the fact that Gods created the heavens and the earth. But this simple change; simple it seems, hides a truth revealed from the beginning of the Torah that it was "Gods" who created the heavens and the earth, not "God".

Without the knowledge of Melchizedek as God's priest, the order of Melchizedek has no effect in our lives as believers and even though we know there is power in the name of Jesus, it still remains that not knowing why there is power in Jesus name limits us in ways unimaginable. But thanks be to God who has given us total victory with the order of Melchizedek, for even the angels must of necessity worship us, for Jesus is the head and we are his body, if they must worship him, they must worship us, but without the knowledge of this, we would be amazed why some demons resist even after we cast them out. But knowing you know the order, they must obey you in the name of Jesus. What you read of Jesus in the Bible, you read of you. Do you believe this? He became as much superior to the angels, as the name he has inherited is superior to theirs. Amen. You are superior to the angels of God, **you are *Gods***.

We have dwelt far too long with our minds on the seen realm of the earth; it is time to live forth from the unseen realm of this world, commanding the powers that be in the heavens above and on the earth beneath the heavens. And if I may add, when God gives you a word, only believe, he means just that, only BELIEVE. He is not asking you to pray about it, he is only asking that you believe because as far as he is concerned, it is fixed. What word has he given you today? Only believe.

Ever since I understood the person of Melchizedek, it's hard to go through the scripture and not marvel at the unseen events that correspond with our present day, how a "man" of the earth came to be a priest in heaven, directly after the command of the heavenly priest Melchizedek. Its lofty thought elevates men to share a knowledge common among angels and ghosts alike. We've been raised far above principalities and powers and seated in Christ at the right hand of the Most-high God.

In my thoughts, I realize how important it is for man to believe in the existence of God; it gives hope for the now and confidence for the future after death. To believe in the unseen and to trust in a God we perceive in our minds is one of the greatest gifts bequeathed to man. I pray we all see this "God" for who he really is.

Jesus said, "But when the Spirit of truth comes, he shall lead you into all truth, he shall not speak of his own, but whatsoever he hears, that shall he tell you, he will take of mine and make it known to you, I say so because all that the father has is mine..." Worthy of note is, "He shall not speak of his own, but whatsoever he hears that shall he speak." Even God's own spirit waits to hear the voice of Jesus, thus, it is obvious he takes instructions from Jesus, but then he further says, "He will take of mine and make it known to you...all that the father has is mine..." Here, Jesus lets us know the words he speaks are the Father's but the books let us know, Jesus does not speak of his own authority as well, for in heaven, he "is a priest after the order of Melchizedek". Thus it is obvious; Jesus himself takes orders from the Father through the priest of the father, who is Melchizedek.

In the Godhead, the two become one; this is a mystery which is why they chose to make man in the image and likeness of the two. They vested of themselves in one entity called man which is who we are, mankind; male and female.

Chapter Three

The Mother: Heaven's Best Kept Secret

"And Gods said, 'Let us make man in our Image, after our likeness...So Gods created man in the image of Gods. In the image of Gods, he created him; male and female he created them" (Genesis 1: 26, 27)

The Bible says, "In the beginning, Gods created the heaven and the earth... Then Gods said, "Let us make man in our image, after our likeness..." (Genesis 1:1,26); So Gods created man in "his" image, man was created male and female, in the image of the Godhead, male and female. Just as the Godhead is two persons, even so, man was made two persons. (Genesis 2), male and female, this is plainly because the Godhead is male and female. The reason the king is referred to as father is because Melchizedek is female and also the mother of all creation. The invisible things of God are clearly seen being understood through the things that have been made. (Romans 1:18-20). Look around you. How many species of mankind do you see? It is clearly two, and the two are male and female, in the image of Elohim.

After whom did Elohim model Eve? He created them male and female, in the image of Elohim. The referred verse implies Elohim is male and female. I have listened to some preachers say Eve was not part of Gods plan or she was made as an afterthought. They fail to reckon that Eve not only was a part of Gods plan, she was also modeled after an existing model, just as Adam was modeled after the Father.

Elohim said to one another, "Let us make man in our image, after our likeness." When the word man is used, it refers to the male and female specie of humans, even so, when the word God is used in the Bible, it could refer to either of these two Gods, the king or his priest. Man is made in the image of the Father, while the woman is made in the image of Melchizedek, for Gods created man in the image of Gods, male and female. And for the purpose of this book and the understanding it serves, we may refer to Melchizedek as the mother.

We are born of Gods and we have overcome the world through spiritual birth, we have been brought by grace into the family of Elohim and the order and command of Melchizedek as the mother of all, with Jehovah as our Father, with Jesus, our brother and high priest. We have received the spirit of the father into our spirits, so we cry to him, calling him father who is the father of spirits. We are not without complete spiritual parenting.

Melchizedek is the mother of all living, both visible and invisible, the father is the father of all living, both visible and invisible, and by the Father, "the whole family in heaven and on earth derives its name" (Ephesians 3:15). There is no way we can completely fathom how the

Godhead created the heavens and the earth through the spoken word. It is like trying to understand the power behind the sperm and the ovum in the conception and eventual delivery of a human child. We may know the process, but not the power, for it is concealed and is only known by God. There have been erroneous teachings that Eve was a by-product of Elohim, that she was created as an afterthought. This is a lie. Man is male and female; Adam was fashioned after the image of the Father, who is only one part of the Elohim, Eve, the female, was fashioned after the second person of the Elohim. Eve is fashioned in image like unto the priest, Melchizedek. This we know because Elohim created Adam and Eve after the very image of the Father and I'd use the term, the "Mother". Jesus came revealing the king as the Father, he said, "I have much more to say to you, but you cannot bear them now, however when he, the spirit of truth comes, he will lead you into all truth..." Melchizedek is the only one revealed to be without beginning of either days or an end of life as clearly written in the book of Hebrews and sits at the right hand of the Father.

Yes, indeed Mary had a son for the Gods and as she gave birth on earth, while in heaven, between Jehovah and Melchizedek, one said to the other, "Unto us, a child is born, unto us, a son is given, and the government shall be upon his shoulder, etc." The government referred to is both of the heavens and the earth. This statement prophesied by the prophet Isaiah, speaks of the events that transpired in heaven upon Jesus' birth on earth. There goes the first surrogate mum and one for the Gods at that. We know the truth and have you ever wondered why the human female also says, "God made us in his image?" We know he said, "Let us make man (humans) in our image, after our likeness" so you better ask yourself this question: Why is it we have only a male and a female man? Search the scriptures for truth. The first century Catholic (universal) church from which stems the present day Roman Catholic Church laid the foundational doctrine and by the 4th century, we had the creed et al. It is noteworthy to reckon the Roman Catholic Church believes in the "mother" of heaven, though I reckon it is a perversion of the true state due to lost and/or stored up books in the library of the Vatican, for surely material exists which affirm the truth of the trinity, which trinity in itself is not a doctrine become true but rather truth become doctrine.

The mystery of God in three persons is unveiled as we have a broader understanding of the books; I would rather remain a priest in the order of Melchizedek, the true and eternal priest of heaven, who is also God and second person of the Godhead, after whose image Eve was made, than be the greatest preacher of our time. Forget the theatrics of most preachers; most of what we have been taught is naught. Melchizedek is the Jerusalem from above and she is our mother, just as the Apostle Paul says to the Galatians in Chapter 4:26, "But the Jerusalem above is free and she is our mother."

Melchizedek is the only one in scripture revealed to be "without beginning of days or end of life" (Hebrews 7:3). Eternally immortal just as the father, Melchizedek is the priest of the Most-high God and her place is by the right hand of the Father, who is the Most-high God. Presently, she gave up her place for Jesus, the son of the Godhead, to sit at the right hand of the father until his enemies are made a footstool for his feet. Once death, the last enemy is swallowed up by immortality in all, Jesus will give back the authority at the right hand to the one who handed it to him and come to rule on earth as high priest after the order of Melchizedek.

Melchizedek brought grace to mankind, just as a mother brings grace to her children from the wrath of the father. Jesus said, "I have so much more to say to you, but you cannot bear it now, but when the spirit of truth comes, he will lead you into all truth..." This grace was first put into effect in meeting with Abraham but its manifestation would not be seen until the resurrection of Jesus and grace only holds the wrath of the father for a time only. Just for the time, Jesus sits at the right hand of the Father and when the time of grace is up, then comes the Father's judgment. Jesus presently occupies the right hand for a while only, for he must give up that place to its rightful owner, which is Melchizedek. How do we know this? It is very clear from the words of the Father. Psalm 110:1 says; The Lord says to my Lord: "Sit at my right hand until I make your enemies a footstool for your feet." His place at the right hand is conditional. The Father says, sit here UNTIL... He is to sit at the right hand only until the time of grace allowed by the priest for the right hand of the Father is the right hand of grace and the place of truth.

Jesus in heaven is the head of the church, we on earth are his body, and he is, along with we who believe in him, a priest after the order (command) of Melchizedek. It has always been two Gods speaking from the beginning; the father speaks judgment, Melchizedek speaks grace, and the time of grace from the Godhead is near over, judgment is coming to the church. We are the offspring of the Godhead and the time for our reprove has come, we must give account, more so for the grace that has been given to us, we shall all stand before the judgment seat of Elohim, though it has been granted us by Elohim to judge angels and we will judge them. (1 Corinthians 6:3)

26 The last enemy to be destroyed is death.27 For he "has put everything under his feet. Now when it says that "everything" has been put under him, it is clear that this does not include God himself, who put everything under Christ.28 When he has done this, then the Son himself will be made subject to him who put everything under him, so that God may be all in all. (1 Corinthians 15:26-28)

Several scholars of theology and the Bible have postulated there are two Gods of the Bible, the God of the Old Testament and the God of the New Testament. They are not far from the truth for with the Old Testament, the Father's judgment ruled over all men while in the New Testament, the mothers grace reigns, the grace that comes through Jesus, who is high priest forever after the order of Melchizedek. Man was created in the Image of the Godhead; first, Adam in the image of the father, Jehovah, and Eve in the image of Melchizedek, who is the priest of the father. Jesus said, "I have so many things to say to you, but you cannot bear them now..." These words are true; he keeps referring to the king as the father because there is a mother. While on earth, he only revealed to us the Father and he said he yet had so many things to say. Imagine the wrath and judgments of the father when the grace of the mother is over. "It is a fearful thing to fall into the hand of the living God..." (Hebrews 10:31)

Needless to say, what was true then in the beginning is true now. When Gods said, "Let us make Man in our own image, after our likeness, and let them rule..." The same is accomplished in Christ and just as the Gods, even so are we in Christ, male and female. Now someone would say, "In Christ there is neither male nor female." Read your Bible better and in context. The order of Melchizedek makes us not only equal to God, it makes us Gods. If we lived in Jesus' day, we who believe will all be killed, for we believe we are the sons of God and that is considered heresy by many even in these times we live in.

The problem with us who believe in Jesus is we want to be "normal", we don't want to be seen as delusional but it is outright delusion to believe in a God you cannot see. It's high time we accept who we really are and care less what the world or anyone thinks about us! We are "believers"; we believe and therefore speak. Someone once said, "It is that which is alive that is in danger of dying," that which is dead is dead. Having been revived in Christ, we ought to stay alive in spirit. For it is we who are alive in Christ that are in danger of death and immortal separation, not they who stand in flesh, condemned already in spirit. The struggle for the soul of man continues, only this time, it's self against the self and self-wins. Most of us who believe are too shallow in mind and slow of heart to believe God's word. We are held hostage by tradition and the doctrines of men; these have contained us to think within the "box" (traditions of men). It is time to break through the veil that conceals the invisible presence from us that we may access all that the great invisible king and his priest have given to us. In your walk with God, you get to a point where you first believe, know, and then perceive the invisible presence of the spirit who leads you. The world thinks we're stupid believing in a God we do not see but that's the very essence of faith; it is the substance of things hoped for and the evidence of things unseen. Faith says the fact you believe in an invisible God proves the invisible God exists, just as we do not see gravity, but facts prove it's keeping us on the ground; else we'd all be flying in the air. Choose to believe. In your past lies a key your future needs, get those keys and unlock the future.

The Father is the Most-high God because there are other Gods he is higher than. These things we teach and we get great results. In my walk with Spirit, I have gained the point where I know I am never alone, the unseen guiding presence is always present. Jesus said, *"When the Spirit of truth comes, he will be with you and in you forever..."* If you ever received God's unseen Spirit, all you have got to do is only believe the words of Jesus above, and experience the presence., I guarantee, faith works better than magic. Apparently, we are not in control of events in our lives, there's a higher power at work. And I will add this here, the name Melchizedek is not just a name, it is actually a title. The holder of the title is the ruler of righteousness and enforcer of peace and today, Jesus is a priest after the order of the one who holds the title "Melchizedek" and that "one" is the "Mother" just as the Father has a title of the "Almighty".

I will bring the blind by a way they knew not, I will lead them in paths that they have not known. I will make darkness light before them and crooked things straight.

These things will I do unto them; I will not forsake them..."
(Isaiah 42:16 KJV)

Chapter Four

Lessons In History

"Do not cast your pearls before pigs, else they will trample on them, and afterward, turn and tear you to pieces..." – Jesus

As a result of diligent comparative study of scripture, this chapter is a compilation of thoughts and beliefs as touching diverse issues entirely to do with the universe, the way of life of the spirits and the societal environs of heaven and its lower realm of earth. Having read so far, if you do not quite believe, you might as well proceed no further and thus enjoy your own opinion, but do not hinder another that would by these encourage himself in virtue and in the knowledge of God.

Everyone may read the Bible and speak as he pleases, it's a right and a privilege to all, for talk is free and mental assent is permissible as the prophet Isaiah tells it but to the initiate, the ability of spirit expressed lies in the theology unearthed from within the books and theology does differ in quality, for many a belief we hold onto, not only have no theological basis and though having high moral values are bereft of spiritual power and value... *"Thinking them to be wise, they became fools and exchanged the glory of the incorruptible God into an image made like corruptible man, birds, and reptiles and creeping things... If any think himself to be wise by this world's standards, let him become a fool, that he may be wise..."*

The General Assembly

Here, we shall look into the general assembly [the entire citizens of Zion], over whom Melchizedek presides as priest of the Most-high and mighty God beginning with the elders of Zion.

The Elders of Zion

Of the elder gods of Zion, little is known about them. Twenty-four in all (Rev. 4:4) these constitute Gods very own heavenly Sanhedrin; they presently are in Zion, the living city of God .

In appearance, they are clothed about in white garments, with gold crowns on their heads; they sit on thrones in the presence of God. But there is something spectacular about the way John describes them in Revelation, he calls them elders. According to the original writings of the Greek New Testament, the word "elders" as used by the translators of the Authorized Version originally read to imply "older persons", which is its synonym.

John calls them older persons/elders because being in the presence of God; he observed something distinct in appearance between them and God who was seated on the throne. He observed in appearance they looked facially older than God and so he readily termed them "older persons/elders". This is just one aspect of what I call the concept of immortality which exists among spirits.

As elders, they bear a unique authority and are relative to the carrying out of several activities in the universe. They have lived as far back as before God by His spirit created any angel, cherub or seraph. They are the elders of God and are subject to Melchizedek's authority, these are the elder gods. Psalm 82:1 says, "God stands in the midst of the mighty, he judges among the gods." These are the gods referred to, we know Melchizedek is without father or mother or genealogy, without beginning of days, or end of life and lives forever. In light of these attributes, Melchizedek is a God, Priest of the Most-high God, and the only other person revealed to be eternally immortal in the Bible, and those who further qualify are the twenty-four elder gods from Revelation chapter 4 onwards. Yet, they worship the lamb because the order of Melchizedek in the book of Hebrews says, "Let all the angels of God, worship him." This order was to the angels but also in Psalm 97: 7, it says "Worship him, all you gods." This particular command of Melchizedek was to the twenty-four elder gods and this is why the elder gods also worship Jesus in heaven.

The Angels

Angels are messengers in divine service to God; created for his glory they constitute a vast majority of the citizens of Zion. From the scriptures, we understand they wear clothes; white garments to be exact, even the twenty-four elders are clothed in white garments (Rev. 4:4). (Obviously these garments are made, for surely the angels were not created with these clothes on). From Daniel's description in Chapter 10 we know they stand as men do and do not have wings contrary to popular belief. They have eyes red as flame with faces that shine like lightning (indeed their faces are luminous and emit white light), feet that gleam like burnished bronze and bodies like chrysolite. Their voices vary from angel to angel, the one spoken of in Chapter 10 had a voice like that of a multitude, whilst the ones in Chapter 8 and 9 including Gabriel, the angel mentioned there, had a voice like that of a man's voice. Letting us know they vary one to another, each being uniquely created by God. From scripture (Psalm 78: 24-25), we know they do eat the grain of heaven as against the grains of the earth (for just as there are edible grains of the earth so are there grains of heaven suitable for eating).

From the word of God, we know they do not have wings for they wear long robes (if they did have wings, Daniel would have written it down and anyway their clothes would obstruct wings protruding from their backs). In no portion of scripture are angels said to have wings. In Rev.14:6, John says, *"And I saw another angel flying in mid-air proclaiming the eternal gospel"*. Not necessarily meaning he had wings. The angel in Daniel Chapter 10 stood over the waters speaking to Daniel, he was not standing on the waters but was hovering over it right up to the end of Chapter 12 and the scripture does not say he had wings.

Angels have the ability to take on the form of men as we see in the destruction of Sodom and Gomorrah. They can have contact with things natural to men such as the angel in John 5:3 who normally comes down to stir up the waters for healing and from what we know they can be with you right now even as you read this book. Angels are incorporeal so they can be with us like the Holy Ghost without our being able to see and touch them. They have been sent to minister to us the heirs of salvation not for a while but for all eternity. In the city of God, there are those amongst them whose duty is to burn incense before Him [Rev. 8:3]; Michael the Archangel is a warrior, a fighter by creation. The book of Revelation 14 tells us of the one who has charge of the fire at the altar of God and Chapter 16 tells us of the one who has charge of the waters of the earth. Each angel has a designated area of responsibility which is his jurisdiction and is expected to operate within the confines of it. Some men amongst us have probably entertained angels unaware. These beings of God possess strength that comes natural to them, highly intellectual beings; they only seek the glory of their God and King. These too are subject to Melchizedek's authority.

The Cherubim

In writing to the Hebrew Christians in Heb. 9:5, the apostle says "… and over it the cherubim of Glory shadowing the mercy seat of which we cannot now speak particularly…" Desiring to teach the recipients of the letter about the cherubim, he found they were not ready for what he had termed strong meat though he had previously gone on to explain to them the person of Melchizedek, but of the cherubim he said he could not now speak particularly for they would not yet comprehend much of what he would have said for of all the creations of God according to revealed scripture, these probably are the most unique of beings.

The first ones to be introduced to us in Genesis 3:24, God placed a few of them wielding Immortal swords to guard the way to the tree of life. For a long while they have been taken for angels but the scripture calls them by the name cherubim. Towering averagely above man in height, the cherubs stand erect on straight legs as men do but with tremendous differences in appearance. First we understand they have got the front and back side as we do but they have a head with four faces, the face in front being the face of a cherub while the one directly opposite it facing the back is the face of a lion, to the right side is the face of a man and to the left the face of an eagle as written in Ezekiel 10:13-14. With the face of a cherub being the face of an ox and rightly so for it matches the feet of a cherub whose feet is the cloven hoofs of an ox (Ezek. 1:7). They are said to have four wings on their backs directly under the face of a lion with eyes all over their wings, under their wings, on their bodies and arms. They see in all directions and are able to move in any way without turning as they go, moving back and forth like flashes of lightning. We know they do talk and like the angels indeed vary one to another, each possessing certain gifts and abilities within them. These cherubs will presently be found in Zion, the city of the living God. They have been given the honor of being royal guards to our God and King. They do not wear clothes as the angels do but are covered by God's glory and feel no shame as Adam was at the creation of man. Satan, once called Lucifer, belongs to this class of beings for Ezekiel 28:14 declares him to be a cherubim and not an angel as assumed by many though he sometimes transforms into an angel of light. (2 Corinthians 11:14) The truth remains that once a cherub, always a cherub for the scripture clearly reveals so. For those of us with curious minds, the face of a cherub being the face of an ox has all the features of the ungulate.

The Seraphim

Little is known concerning the seraphim for God has thought it fit to be so. One can only imagine what they look like if the cherubim appear as revealed in the scriptures. The only place they are mentioned is in Isaiah Chapter six where by God's word their faces and feet were not seen by the prophet thus keeping also from us the knowledge of what they look like. We only know they have six wings on their backs and they talk, having also two hands as the cherub do. The rest is better left to the imagination. Together, these people constitute the entire populace of the spiritual city of Zion over whom Melchizedek is priest and some day we will all see them in their true self and not see them darkly through a glass (the word of God) as it were.

The Nephilim

"...and the sons of Gods saw the daughters of men that they were beautiful, and they married any of them they chose... **The Nephilim were on the earth in those days,** *and also, after the sons of Gods went to the daughters of men and had children by them, their children became heroes, men of renown." (Genesis 6:2, 4)*

Most times when we read this portion, we mistake the children of the watchers for the Nephilim but a careful study shows the reference to the Nephilim was a different issue entirely and was just to let us know the Nephilim were already on earth in those days when the Angels sinned through lust for women. Who then are the Nephilim?

The Hebrew root meaning for the word Nephilim, is "cast out ones, or outcasts", so the verse above reads, "the outcasts were on earth in those days..." letting us know that even before the angels sinned, the outcasts were already on earth. The scriptures let us know Lucifer aka Satan and his angels were cast down to the earth after their rebellion in heaven long before Adam was created. These are the Nephilim; the cast out ones, the outcasts of heaven, the renegade spirits on earth whose origins are from above and who presently also oppress the earth and its inhabitants. So next time you're asked who the Nephillim are? Impart knowledge.

The Abominable Offspring of Angels and Women

Genesis tells us of the children born to the fallen angels. We know that even though their origin is celestial, they remain terrestrial spirits for they were born of mankind. This was a race not created by God but created through the union of spirits and men. They were male and female but obviously drowned in the flood. It was actually evil wrought by them on the earth that gave cause for the flood. The Bible says evil increased on the earth in those days. These drowned in the flood but roam the earth as wicked spirits in the unseen heavenly realm of the earth. Paul identified them in saying "... and against wicked spirits in the heavenly realm." These hate believers for its our Father God who caused the flood that killed them and also Imprisoned their fathers in the darkness of hell just as Peter and Jude tell us of "... the angels who kept not their first estate but abandoned them, these he has reserved in chains of darkness..."

The children born to the angels that sinned in the days of Noah were not just men; they were a breed even God did not create. The fathers were immortal spirits, while their mothers were mortal and human. The angels had children, male and female children from women of the earth. We are not told if the children also had other children, but considering the length of days at the time, this is probable. These children of mixed origin (celestial and terrestrial) all died in the flood. The flood was actually a result of their wicked practices. Now upon their death, these spirits obviously cannot ascend to heaven for they are terrestrial spirits for they were born on earth even though their origins were celestial. These still roam the earth and are both male and female spirits; the offspring of the unholy union between angels and earthly women. They are full of wrath and anger toward Elohim and believers; this is so because God not only punished their fathers by jailing them, he is also responsible for their earthly death.

There you have it, the Incubus and Succubus, male and female spirits who lay claim to men and women for they know your ancestral bloodlines.

The Concept of Immortality

*"In the beginning O lord, you laid the foundations of the earth, and the Heavens are the work of your hands. They will perish, but you remain; they will wear out like a garment. You will roll them up like a robe; like a garment they will be changed. **But you remain the same and your years will never end.**" (Hebrews 1:10-12 NIV)*

The concept of immortality among spirits is the ability to live continuously, adding years and yet not subject to outward aging in appearance, sickness or death, etc. It is the ability to keep growing older even for a thousand years and keep looking the same as at when you first lived immortal and/or were created.

In Christ, men are granted immortality which is the ability to live forever and not grow old in appearance and not die. Its consummation is in the resurrection. We have a promise from God, we believe and we shall see that which we believe. Add to immortality, the promises in the book of Revelation:

1. The crown of life.

2. The right to feed from the tree of life.

3. Receiving some of the hidden manna and a new name.

4. Receive authority over the nations.

5. Be dressed in white with names in the book of life.

6. Made a staunch pillar in the temple of God.

7. The right to sit with God.

What you get is men become Gods. This is the promise of God in Revelation to men and someone will say we are wrong to profess we are Gods? Oh please.

The Concept of Adaptation

"Do not forget to entertain strangers, for by doing so some people have entertained angels without knowing it." *(Hebrews 13:2 NIV)*

As it was in the beginning even so is it now. The Bible teaches us in several places where angels appeared in human form visiting men. We have such records even about Abraham being visited by men who turned out to be angels and the Lord inclusive. Melchizedek appeared in human form, perhaps as a man to Abraham, and yet we are told in the verses quoted above to entertain strangers, for in so doing, many have entertained angels without knowing. It is still happening today just as it was in Bible days. This is a clear indication that even in our day; spirits still appear in human form and walk amongst us as men and women. What better way to walk amongst men unnoticed than to look as one of them? I refer to this as the spiritual concept of adaptation. The watchers are ever present, be conscious of this knowledge for they make notes of all the activities of all men; the very same notes by which you will be judged for all the things done while you once lived in your body though afterwards dead and separate from it. They are not called watchers for nothing; they watch you, even now!

Angels do have the ability to transform to humans. It is the concept of adaptation. This is the ability to adapt to any form on the planet earth. But they are unable to do so in heaven. The reason they can shape shift is because the earth is a lower realm of existence. As said before, Hebrews 13:4 tells us; "Do not forget to entertain strangers, for in so doing many has entertained angels without knowing it..." This is a message for the now; as it was in the beginning, so it is now. It has always been so, and yes, when transformed to human form, they also relish everything man enjoys. I have two encounters of such. The first being around 3 am on February 3rd, 2015 and this was an experience I will not forget. Those to whom I have shared know the story.

Qualities of a True Deity (Hebrews 7:3)

1. Without father, without mother, without descent

2. Without beginning of either day or an end of life

3. Lives forever

Qualities of Men Divinized to become Gods (Hebrews 1:10-12)

1. Remain the same (in appearance)

2. Years shall not end (live forever)

The Book of Truth

*"So he said to me, "Do you know why I have come to you? Soon I will return to fight against the prince of Persia, and when I go, the prince of Greece will come, **but first I will tell you what is written in the Book of Truth...**" (Daniel 10:20-21 NIV)*

In response to Daniel's petitions toward heaven, an angel was sent to give him understanding of all that was yet to happen both to the children of Israel and the world at large. Further reading of the above scripture implies the angel is speaking about future events yet to take place on the earth but the angel references a hitherto unknown book in heaven. He calls it the Book of Truth from which he informs Daniel about events yet to take place on the earth. We are familiar with the Book of Life, which is in itself a book with recorded names of those who overcome and believe till their last breath on earth, but the Book of Truth is Gods record of all earthly events from the foundation of the world to the last day of the judgment and probably into the future. It is no wonder our days are numbered in this Book of Truth and as such we trust the Lord that which he has begun in our lives, he is able and faithful to perfect it for it is all written in his Book of Truth. Lord, teach us to number our days aright according to the words of the Book of Truth in heaven, Amen. When God calls a man, he reads it from the Book of Truth in heaven. You are being read; it's your time to rise and shine. Just as he read to Jeremiah, *"Before I formed you in your mother's womb, I knew you and ordained you a prophet to the nations..."* he is reading your call. We have been sent to reveal the secrets of the heavens above which are invisible and perceived by faith and the invisible secrets of the Earth beneath the heavens.

Whatever happens in your life is all a part of that which God has written in his book. Always have faith, "for without faith it is impossible to please God..." We live our lives from Gods word written in the Book of Truth which is in heaven.

Eternity: Heaven's Time Frame

It has been said that in the realm of spirits there is neither time nor distance but this is not to be the case as the scriptures reveal for eternity being timeless is not necessarily the absence of time/state of timelessness, but the continuous flow of time such as cannot be measured as proved by man's inability to comprehend its origin/endlessness. To those living in its realms, to God and to spirits alike, it is time uninterrupted by neither day nor night; it is time without the dictates of the sun or moon, indeed it is time without end. Eternity so far being constant can only be measured as was (past), is (present) and is to come (future) by its activities as evidenced in the scripture for God does indeed live in a state of time where there is an incessant flow of activity.

By faith we understand that before the worlds were framed at Gods command, He is and with Him is Melchizedek His priest. By faith, we also understand they lived millennia before each cherubim was created, or an angel was ever given a name, or mountains seen were made or the rivers of the earth did flow, long before the cherubim Lucifer made the devil of himself, or before he ever thought in his heart to rebel against the Most-high. Indeed, the Godhead pre-exist what we know to be the beginning and have long lived in this realm of time called eternity, knowing in themselves details of the whole truth unknown to man such as the creation of cherubs and also knowing the exact length of days from Genesis till date proving as earlier said the existence of time in this unseen realm of the universe. For truly, in heaven time does exist and can only be measured by its flood of activities as seen in the creation of angels down onto the sixth day and creation of man in his present state and surely God knows he did not create Adam in this present millennium we live in but rather as scripture proves a few millennia ago. All spirit beings as well as the just departed souls of men we have known, function in this realm of time and are governed by eternity's continuous flow, Zion inclusive in its endless day as each angel goes about his dealing. The point of all now said is the existence of time as eternity in the unseen realm of the universe and that in a state of uninterrupted flow.

Mount Zion and Its Summit

In the unseen realm of the universe, according to revealed scripture, are the heights of Mount Zion, a mountain in the spiritual realm, unseen and hidden from the eyes of men but revealed to be the dwelling place of God. On its northern summit stands the heavenly Jerusalem, the city of the living God in all its glory with the clouds of God around the mountain peaks. In the unseen realm of heaven are mountains, numerous and glorious to behold, one of whom is Mount Zion with its rocky crags just as you would find on the mountains of the earth. With imposing stature, this is the mountain the Lord has chosen to dwell for all eternity and all its glory we shall see when we go from here to be with our God.

Zion: Its Rivers and Trees

On the heights of Mount Zion, in the city of God flows the river of the water of life down the middle of the great street, with the tree of life on either side of it yielding its fruit in its season (Rev. 22:1). Psalm 46:3 truly tells us there is a river whose streams indeed make glad the city of God where the Most-high dwells. It is a river whose waters flow like the waters of the rivers of the earth with the difference being that it is of the higher realm of life. Though unstable as the waters of the earth, its pure streams indeed make glad the city of God for it is water whose springs are of life (read the account of Lazarus and the rich man and understand that as spirit he (the rich man) needed water to quell his torment in hell for celestial beings (spirits) also utilize water as an element in their realm, (Luke 16:19-31). These waters and the tree of life amongst other trees have existed long before the earth was created, a wonder amid Gods creations in the celestial realm of the universe with the fruit of the trees being very much edible. As "Gods" (celestial beings) having being resurrected, we the church of God will eat from this tree of life that is in the midst of the paradise of God on either side of the river of the water of life for in Zion, the living city of God, and indeed the whole universe, celestial beings do eat as men do. The scripture reveals to us that for forty years, God fed the children of Israel with "manna", which is revealed in scripture as the food of angels, even the grain of heaven as opposed to the grain of earth. For God having created Adam in His own image who at the time knew no sin, gave him every seed bearing plant on the whole earth and every fruit tree with seed in it for food (Genesis 1:29) because as the creator so is the creation.

Zion: Immortal Blades and Living Garments

So He drove out the man and he placed at the east of the Garden of Eden cherubim and a flaming sword, which turned every way to keep the way to the tree of life. (Genesis 3:24)

The above scripture from the book of beginnings says God placed cherubim wielding flaming sword to guard the way to the tree of life. Let us observe and understand the scripture is clear in its choice of words. If it says swords, it is because they had swords with them, and if they had swords at that time, they still do to this day, and if they do it is because there are swords in the realm of celestial creatures and these swords are made for surely they did not come into being of themselves. And just as the axe cannot raise itself against its' bearer, so also these swords unless wielded cannot turn everyway nor flash back and forth for indeed it is the cherubim who are able to flash back and forth and move in every way as is written in Ezekiel 1:12,14.

Speaking of angels and clothes, in many passages of scripture, whenever they are described, the angels are dressed in living garments of white linen, as do the elders, the high-priest Jesus and also our God. For in the heavenly realm, not only do they wear clothes as men do, in my opinion these clothes are made for surely they did not spin into being of themselves but rather were spun into reality. And we Christians, when we leave this world to be with our God, having been raised from the dead (not as men but as Gods - Sons of God Almighty) will also be given white robes to wear for celestial beings according to revealed scripture wear clothes as men do.

Zion: Golden Censers; Incense and Smoke

"And another angel came and stood at the altar, having a <u>golden censer</u>, and there was given unto him much <u>incense</u>, that he should offer it with the prayers of all saints upon the <u>golden altar</u> which was before the throne. And the <u>smoke</u> of the incense, which came with the prayers of the saints, ascended up before God out of the angel's hand. (Revelation 8:3, 4; emphasis added)

From the above scripture, I believe it is quite clear to all that in the spiritual city of Zion not only is incense offered onto God with its smoke rising before Him, if it must be offered, it must be done with golden censers by the angels whose charge it is to burn incense before God. As we know it on earth, there is smoke stemming from incense being burned in golden censers swung from the hands of angels as often as required in the presence of God almighty. In other words - in the heavenly realm, not necessarily in the city of God, there is smoke as we know it on earth, such whose fragrance can either be sweet smelling or repulsive and is able to dissolve into nothing.

Heaven's Own Hierarchy

1. The Father, Jehovah.

2 The Father's priest, Melchizedek

3. The Son, Jesus (King and Priest)

This is the true trinity of the Christian faith and they live forever along with the spirits of just men made perfect.

4. The General Assembly; 24 elder gods, angels, seraphs, cherubs

All things have been put under man. In the resurrection, men are made Gods and we will rule over all spirits. We will not be men, we will be Gods. Now, are we the sons of God though we do not look it? But at the resurrection, not only will we be Gods, we will look it. St. Paul says, "As there is a natural body, there is also a spiritual body." These things we believe and we receive by faith. He came, not to die for the righteous, but for us who know in us, we can do nothing against the truth but only for the truth.

Who Speaks Through You?

Jesus said, *"The words I speak are not mine but the father's."* He went on to say, *"Abraham rejoiced to see my day....Before Abraham was, I am."*

Who spoke, was it Jesus, the son of man speaking, or the spirit of the Father speaking through him at the time? For before Abraham was, the spirit did exist and Jesus, the son of man, was born circa 2000 years ago. Who speaks? Are you the one speaking or the spirit in you speaking through you? Both speak at different times. Jesus said, *"...take no thought what you shall say, for in that moment it will be given you what to say, for **it is not you** who will be speaking, **but the spirit of your father speaking through you...**"* I now ask a question. When Jesus said, *"Before Abraham was, I am,"* who spoke? Was it Jesus the man, or the spirit of the father speaking through Jesus the man?

Walking with Jesus

To follow Jesus is not necessarily to walk in the path he walked, none can. To follow Jesus is to walk in the path he "leads" you in, not necessarily beside still waters, which was David's path but surely in the path of righteousness. The path Jesus walked was to die for mankind; you must find your path as he leads you for in your path lays your true purpose. Is Jesus leading you? Every man to his path and let the Lord gently lead you quietly.

The path God leads you may not be pleasant ground to walk on, just as he led Jesus on his own path which was death on the cross to redeem mankind. It felt so horrible Jesus prayed, "Father, if it's possible, let this cup pass by, however, not my will, but yours be done..." Here, we understand why Jesus said, when we pray, we make as a point in prayer to God, "lead us not into temptation." For God does this to test and strengthen our faith. The Spirit of God led Jesus to the wilderness to be "tempted of the devil." Your path presently may be strewn with delay, rejection, slander, malice and all evils against you, but one thing is certain, "we know that all things work together for good to those who love God and are called in line with his purpose." You're coming out victorious! Hang in there, help is on the way folks, only believe.

Thoughts of Conscience

Thoughts of conscience are actually conversations between angels and demons vying for the man. Especially as children, the conscience we thought was ours is actually words from either of the two mentioned above, the one refraining us from evil, the other prodding us to do evil, while both stand invisible on the right and left hand. Through our use of the word of righteousness, we can now discern these voices to know between good and evil.

Dreams

Gods do speak to men. In visions and dreams of the night, God does instruct man in the way he should go. Dreams are our consciousness of Gods realm of existence. When we dream, we are in a conscious reality of the realm where spirits exist and unless otherwise proved by God, all dreams take place in the spiritual unseen realm of the earth. When we dream, we are conscious of the reality of the spirit realm. A dream reflects the activities of the spirit realm; dreams are portals that project our consciousness into the realm of spirit. It is as a mirror reflecting to us the spirit realm and its activities. Dreams are reality and are of more substance than the seen physical realm.

Dreams are actually visions of what the spirits are either doing, have done or intend to do. They can refer to heavenly or earthly events. Dreams are also visions of revelation to show you actual earthly events and could refer the past, present or future events here on earth. In a dream, you can see the plans the enemy schemes to execute in the physical realm; it could be an immediate plan, it could be a ten year plan, and God also reveals his plans and thoughts to us through dreams. One sure way of knowing the source of each dream is simple, Jeremiah 29:11 says "I know the thoughts I have towards you, thoughts of good and not evil, to bring you an expected end." The Lord only gives us thoughts of good toward us and these thoughts come in dreams. The enemy delights in giving dreams of evil with a dreadful end. Just as all things work together for good, even so all of God's thoughts toward us are dreams of good and not evil. *"Strong meat belongs to them who through use of the word of righteousness have exercised their senses to discern between good and evil."* (Hebrews 5)

God said of Adam, "It is not good that the man should be alone, I will make him a suitable help." Next thing he does is, put the man to sleep while he forms the woman. Notice, Adam slept while God worked (dreams come in sleep) and as he awakes, he sees a woman. Jesus said, "While men slept, the enemy sowed tares..."

See to it you understand the will of God concerning dreams and prophecy for they go together, dreams prophesy, just as Joel says from God, *"And afterward, I will pour out my spirit on all people. Your sons and daughters will prophesy, your old men will dream dreams, your young men will see visions."* May the Lord help you understand the power of dreams that you may steer your world aright.

In January 2004, I had a dream. Walking on the road with a brother I knew, we moved around preaching the word with Bible in hand when suddenly I heard laughter from a small group beside us. I told the brother, *"Please wait for me, I need to find out why these fellows are laughing at me."* I walked over to them as they sat on a bench. There were four of them, three males and a female. I asked, *"Why are you people laughing at me?"* The male who seemed their leader said, *"Why are you busy doing what you are not supposed to be doing? Or do you want, at 33, people will begin to say, all the money he has been making, where has it been going to?"* Then I responded, "What do you want me to do?" At this, the male shoved the female beside him, motioned me to sit and said, "Sit down and let me explain to you what we are saying." These were demons and in that dream they represented the four elements of life. The following Sunday, I recall going to meet the church secretary where I worshipped at Christ Embassy Ojo, Lagos-Nigeria. Sister Lily looked at me in bewilderment as I sought explanation of the dream which perplexed me. She waived me off as unimportant. The next ten years of my life proved exactly as they had said and today I wish she had been more receptive, perhaps it would have made a difference in my life. I pray the Lord gives us grace to lead those over whom he has placed us.

Angel Money

"And your father hath deceived me, and changed my wages ten times; but God suffered him not to hurt me. If he said thus, the speckled shall be thy wages; then all the cattle bare speckled: and if he said thus, the ringstraked shall be thy hire; then bare all the cattle ringstraked. Thus God hath taken away the cattle of your father, and given them to me. And it came to pass at the time that the cattle conceived, that I lifted up mine eyes, and saw in a dream, and, behold, the rams which leaped upon the cattle were ringstraked, speckled, and grisled. And the angel of God spake unto me IN A DREAM, saying, Jacob: And I said, here am I. And he said, Lift up now thine eyes, and see, all the rams which leap upon the cattle are ringstraked, speckled, and grisled: for I have seen all that Laban doeth unto thee. I am the God of Bethel, where thou anointedst the pillar, and where thou vowedst a vow unto me: now arise, get thee out from this

land, and return unto the land of thy kindred." (Genesis 31:7-13 KJV -Emphasis added)

The above scripture refers to the time of Jacob's deal with Laban concerning his wages. Prior to this deal, the Angel of the Lord had appeared to Jacob in a dream, instructing him on the fact all the cattle will bear the same speckled, ringstraked and grisled offspring, on this premise and believing the word of the Lord from the angel, Jacob made a deal with Laban. First agreeing to take only kids born as ringstraked, while Laban took all speckled and grisled kids but all cattle gave birth to ringstraked. This happened for a while and Laban changed the agreement ten times but every time the cattle would bear exactly as Jacob agreed and thus Jacob became rich and wealthy.

This is what I call angel money; a situation where a man is instructed by God on how to precede in life and business and by obedience to the word spoken, the man becomes wealthy. Further reading shows us that to reinforce his faith, whilst the flocks mated, Jacob would place poplar leaves in the water troughs as they drank. He did this to further embolden his faith in his dream though he was only required to believe the words spoken and act accordingly. He obeyed the word of the Lord and grew rich. God is still in the business of instructing men in righteousness and business. I encourage you to receive angel money.

Faith

By faith we understand the worlds were created at Gods command, such that the visible things we see were made from the invisible we do not see... (Hebrews 11:2)

With faith as little as a mustard seed, you can say to that mountain before you, move and it will obey you, and what you base your faith on and in is most important. The question is, "What" do you believe? Hebrews 11:1 gives us two definitions of faith but most times we read it as one sentence. It says, "Now faith is the substance of things hoped for, AND the evidence of things not seen."

The word now as expressed above implies "first" faith is the assurance of the things we hope and believe for. It is the substance and gives material appearance to the things we expect to see in our lives, it is faith that brings to pass all we desire, believe and hope for. In other words, faith brings about the manifestation of the things we are yet to see. Second, faith is the only proof you ever need for the existence of things invisible and unseen to the eyes. The fact that you believe in a God whom you have never seen and who is concealed from the human senses only proves the existence of that God, this is FAITH. Faith is the only evidence you will ever need to know Jesus rules over all heaven and earth. Your faith is proof enough that he not only rose from the dead but is seated at the right hand of the Father in heaven. Faith is the doctrine of believing, Jesus said, "Only believe" and faith is to you what you perceive it to be, as God is to you what you perceive him to be. Yet, one thing is certain; faith is faith, as God is God, unchanging in nature, ever constant, consistent, and fully self-existent like the law of gravity. The fact you don't see it don't mean it don't exist; it's keeping you on the ground and that's proof enough that gravity exists, even so God! *"The one without the Spirit does not accept the things that come from the Spirit of God, for they are foolishness to him, and he cannot understand them, because they are spiritually discerned."* Even so is faith.

To live by faith, is to live with conscious confident awareness and assured belief that those things delineated in God's word are true and the things testified to by His Spirit are a reality... Only believe! The Word is our resource! Faith has nothing to do with emotions or how you feel. It's got everything to do with simply believing the word of the Lord Irrespective of how you feel or what you think; faith is no respecter of the senses! Faith welcomes you to the world of make believe, a world where all things are possible. Such as the fact that as you read these words, the invisible Holy Spirit of God is standing right next to you, aiding your comprehension and understanding of the very words read; this is faith, to only believe. When God calls you, he gives no map to read for direction, rather, his word is opened to you, be able to discern the time and season of his plan, so you know when it is time to give up fishing fish to fishing men, seek counsel that you be led right, for *"in the multitude of counselors, there is safety"*. It was also hard for the Peters and the Johns to give up fishing but when the time comes, you just know it is, seek guidance at such a time. We live by faith not by sight. There's the truth of it, always make the Lord your strength. He will never leave you nor forsake you, even in times of adversity; he is a sure God and perfects his will in the lives of His own. The same yesterday, today and forever, His word is truth and honor. In our walk with God, there comes a time when faith elevates to trust. At this point, faith really is the foundation we build trust on. We must move from the foundation of faith towards God to trusting in him so like the three Hebrew boys, Shedrach, Meshach and Abednego; who refused to bow down to King Nebuchadnezzar's image, we say, our God is able to deliver us but peradventure he does not, we still would not bow to this Image. This is trust and this is what God desires of each and every one of us.

Of Melchizedek, Abraham and the Tithe

The purpose of Melchizedek meeting with Abraham was to establish an eternal order of sequence, linking spirits and men; a sequence that guarantees the foremost eternal intentions of the Gods, which intention from the very beginning was made known when they said, "Let us make man in our image, after our likeness."

Beyond creating man; male and female, exactly in their own image, man was created gods right in the direct likeness of the creators, who in themselves are male and female, hence man was to be worshipped, and man was to rule over the slaves of the Gods. These slaves consist of angels, cherubs and seraphs, (of which Satan, aka Lucifer is a Cherub). In the past, long ago in eternity's chronicles, a daring slave cherub named Lucifer led a revolt against the Gods and against the elder gods, the latter of whom there are twenty-four of them (see Revelation 4:4). After this rebellion, there was division in the heavens for a civil war ensued between servants loyal to the Gods and elder gods and those of the rebellion. It is in view of this that the Gods chose to make man, only this time man was to be made in the very image of the Gods, both male and female. Now, we all know the story of the fall and all that followed, with the fall; man could not be divinized as was the original intentions of the Gods so they had a plan. Jesus was to be born on earth, a man of flesh and blood. He was to live and be killed once for all men as an eternal sacrifice and afterwards rise in glory from the dead and serve in heaven as priest, ruling over both heaven and earth and thus fulfilling their original intentions. But for this to happen, after resurrection, he must be a priest after the order and command of Melchizedek. Certain requirements had to be met before a man of the earth could serve in heaven's priesthood. Melchizedek being priest in heaven, the one who receives tithes there in heaven (Hebrews 7:8) had to tithe from a man of the earth, thus Abraham was chosen for his faith for he was counted righteous by God. This prompted Melchizedek coming to the earth, most likely in human form and meeting with Abraham. As heaven's high priest, a heavenly ritual had to be done; the giving of bread and wine of the heavens on the part of Melchizedek and another heavenly ritual had to be done on earth by Abraham thus Melchizedek receiving of Abraham one-tenth of the spoils of war.

Please note Abraham gave Melchizedek of the spoils of war, not of his own goods. This significance held because Abraham, a man of earth had gained war victory by the help of God and as a debt gave to God of the spoils of war. This signified the change that would take place with the death, burial and resurrection of Jesus, taking back control of the earth from the rebel slaves of the Gods. This was the first part in purpose for meeting with Abraham because thousands of years later, Abraham's descendant would ascend to heaven and be a priest after the command of Melchizedek, the very same Melchizedek who years before had met with his ancestor on earth and blessed him.

The tithe was a significant ritual. For according to Hebrews 7:8, Melchizedek receives the tithe in heaven; its full import will only be known when we arrive in heaven. We do not presume to hold all the answers but we do affirm that which we know to be true. Regarding the church in these times, and the paying of tithes, I must say that contrary to all that I had been taught and all I once believed, it is not mandatory to pay tithes to churches here on earth. This I know to be true (and I also have the Spirit of God) for Jesus has risen once for all time and now appears before the throne in heaven as our high priest and brother and we also being priests in the order of Melchizedek. Jesus himself does not receive tithes in heaven; Melchizedek tithes the people of heaven. The old system of the law and its ordinances were done away with and we now have a new priesthood in Christ, the Melchizedek Priesthood, and as Levi is said to have paid tithes in Abraham to Melchizedek (Hebrews 7:9), though Levi was a son after the flesh, how much more we who are of the faith of Abraham? We also paid tithe in Abraham to Melchizedek once and for all time. You may keep your conscience intact and do as it behooves you, whether or not we pay tithes, one does not sin for it now becomes a matter of conscience and conviction. In quietness and assurance, we know we are in the light and abide not in the darkness around us.

Chapter Five

Elohim: The Grand Illusionist

"Then both Philip and the eunuch went down into the water and Philip baptized him. When they came up out of the water, the Spirit of the Lord suddenly took Philip away, and the eunuch did not see him again, but went on his way rejoicing. Philip however, appeared at Azotus and travelled about, preaching the gospel in all the towns until he reached Caesarea." (Acts 9:38-40 NIV)

Night falls, as he is seated in the dark room with fellow students at the university, barely lit with a candle and sharing the word of God with colleagues seated before him, apparently it was not a planned meeting for his flat mate, Donatus *(Real name, a twin of Dennis).* Having been sick, he received three friends paying a courtesy visit to wish him well. In a little while, the candle burns out and he goes to buy another stick, alight again and sharing the word of God with those seated, they all notice the candle burning out halfway in less than fifteen minutes. On impulse, he turns pointing toward the candle, saying, "Keep burning but do not consume the wax further." It took over an hour when one of those present, in shock exclamation, points to the candlelight, saying *"Look! The candle is not burning!"*

The earth being one world has two realms to it. The world as you know it is not real. It is a simulation of a reality that exists far above this plane of existence. Hence the illusory nature of the earth portrays an illusion as our reality and the reality as Imagination and dreams and visions. These realms of the earth cannot be separated from one another but with the mind of Christ, we can clearly make a distinction between these two realms of the earth. There is the seen natural realm of the earth and the concealed spiritual (heavenly) realm of the earth.

Our opening scripture verse tells of the meeting between the evangelist, Philip, and the Ethiopian eunuch. Upon baptizing the eunuch and ascending out the river, Philip disappears and is seen no more. Obviously, the eunuch would have gone on to Ethiopia with the report he was met with and baptized by an angel but this was no angel, this was the evangelist, Philip, a man with like passions as we have and yet disappeared as willed by the spirit, only to appear miles away at Azotus. These things still happen today. The seen realm in which we live consists of our environment, the things we see and make contact with. The imperceptible heavenly realm in which we also live is its opposite; it's the realm of celestial creatures and spiritual conflict, concealed and unknown to man. It's the realm around us; in it we live and move and have our being, and it is the realm of the air; the realm we depend on for the breath of life we breathe. That's how much of it we live in; indeed, this realm surrounds us.

The Holy Spirit of God, being celestial in person is of this realm which is why not only is he with us, he is also in us yet we cannot see him or touch him for this concealed realm is the higher realm of the earth. It is spiritual and heavenly in itself, indeed the entire spirit world is with us still such that as you read this book, the Holy Spirit is present with you but you cannot see him nor touch him.

That we wrestle against principalities, against powers, against the rulers of the darkness of this world and against wicked spirits in the heavenly realms does not mean these enemies of ours live in the third heavens above, the dwelling place of God. On the contrary; according to scripture, they were thrown to the earth, and presently they live in men and function in the unseen spiritual (heavenly) realm of the earth which indeed is unseen to our eyes but in which we live.

We cast devils out of men yet some among us teach they live in the heavens above us, others that they are in hell beneath. Not reckoning with scripture that they were thrown to the earth (Ezekiel 28:17). Nowhere in scripture is it written that Satan and his devils are in hell or even had access to hell. The spirits in prison mentioned by Peter (1 Peter 3:17, 2 Peter 2:4) are the angels of God that sinned in the days of Noah taking to themselves wives of the daughters of men. (See Gen. 6:1-4 for these spirits that disobeyed in Noah's day). God remanded them in eternal chains in the darkness of hell's prisons being reserved for judgment on the great day when they would be cast into the lake of fire and brimstone and Jesus, by the Spirit of God, preached to them a message of confirmation, confirming to them Gods word that the seed of the woman would crush the head of the serpent; he (Jesus) being the seed. For at the time Adam fell, these angels of God had not yet sinned so they knew a seed of man would be born who would crush the head of the serpent. These fallen angels are not on earth; rather they are locked up in hell's prisons. The devils on earth are those that sinned in the rebellion and along with Satan were thrown out of the mountain of God to the earth. They live and function in the unseen realm of the earth. Not far away as many like to believe but as close as we casting them out of men, as close amongst men as the Holy Spirit living in us. Functioning in the realm unseen to us, yet with us, we see them through the word of God through the understanding imparted to us by the revelation of Gods Spirit.

As said before, nowhere is it written that Satan and his devils on earth had access to hell for from Gods word we understand hell is the place unrighteous men go after death and in its underground prisons the angels that sinned in the days of Noah are kept apart from the unrighteous men, bound with eternal chains until the day of judgment when we will be given authority to judge them (1 Corinthians 6:3). God will not allow Satan access or even the rule of right to hell for these unfaithful are accountable to him alone as God and they presently are in the custody of angels being reserved for judgment on the great day. So, we see Satan and his devils are not in hell but rather as scripture says are on earth. And neither is Satan allowed access into the holy city of God where as a rebel, in the past, long before Adam was created, along with his cohorts, he once attempted with the ferocity of a cherub to overthrow the Divine God and in the ensuing conflict that followed there was war in heaven. On that day, to the holy angels it was a call to arms in defense of their pride, in defense of their city and in defense of their God and King. Indeed actual fighting took place as they (Satan's angels) tried very hard to break into the city of God and possess control of the mount but they were not strong enough and subsequently lost their place in heaven. They were thrown to the earth after being stripped of their bodies for which reason they are able to inhabit a man. If they must manifest themselves on earth, it can only be done through the agency of a human body for only a spirit without a body of its own can be domiciled in a man, otherwise it is impossible for celestial beings to live in man. Like the Holy Spirit, these devils also live and function in the unseen realm of the earth.

From all this, we reckon the earth has got two realms, the seen earthly realm and the unseen heavenly realm around and with us which is concealed from the mind and knowledge of man, such that to him, knowledge as this is foolishness, but to us who believe it is the wisdom and power of God revealed. Spirits function in the unseen realm around us which is why we cannot see the Holy Spirit who is with us for He functions in this realm of the earth.

These spirit beings can make contact with the seen realm. I mean they could cause seen things to move without us seeing them moving these things like the angel in John 5:3 who normally would stir the waters up for healing. Obviously, the invalids never saw the angel but whenever they saw the waters being stirred, they rushed in that they may be healed. They can mightily influence the actions of men and the course of life. But for us Christians, the Holy Spirit is the influence in our lives; He is our teacher, our guide through life, our counselor and our comforter. We cannot see them but they do see us, though not as we see ourselves do they see us for they do not have human eyes or bodies with which to look out from and see into our realm as we see it so they see the seen realm from the perspective of the unseen realm. Looking at us, they see us as they see themselves - I mean they look upon our spirits just as we look upon our outward selves. They hear us as we hear ourselves only if they are within hearing distance. This applies to all except God for Him alone by his spirit sees and hears everything and everyone at the same time.

The world as we know it is not real. This may shock not quite a few but it remains the truth. We live in an animation of the creators, as though it were real. The earth is fashioned as a copy of the heavens and the earth in all its forms only serves as a ground where men are tested for the eternal glory about to be revealed at the coming of Jesus. The laws governing the earth exist but the reason why blind eyes see, the lame walk, men walking on water and all other sort of paranormal events is simply because the earth is as real only to the extent of which we perceive it. It is a simulation of the heavens. Jesus came speaking to the wind and the waves and they obeyed him, not just because he was God but because he knew the laws governing the earth. The same applied to the apostles and to this day, all that is needed is an understanding of the earth and its existent realms. In my previous book, *The Person of Melchizedek*, I talked about the earth having two realms, the seen realm which consists of all that is perceptible to the senses and the unseen realm of the earth which harbors the spirits that live here on earth with men, such as the Holy Spirit who is not only in you, but also with you as you read this, walking beside you everywhere you go. This, the word of God teaches us and all we need do is believe. Our minds need to perceive the reality and existence of the unseen realm of the earth, only then can we comprehend the true state of the world we live in and understand why miracles do happen and other such things as are not commonplace amongst men. The devils are not in hell, they are here on earth and live in men amongst us; they are so close and we cast them out of men! Understand they are not in hell; they live inside the bodies of men. When it comes to God and his word, his knowledge gives you authority; his Spirit is your power.

Chapter Six

Ye Are Gods

"They know not, neither do they understand, the foundations of the earth are out of course, I have said, Ye are gods, and all of you are children of the Most-high God, but ye shall die like mere men, and fall like one of the princes..." *(Psalm 82:6)*

I recall a vision of the night sometime in late 2001. As I lay on a bed seemingly afloat a river, there appeared around the bed several books on the river surface. I was seeking which book to delve into and suddenly I caught a Bible amongst the many books around. On its cover page had the words, *"Go Deep"*, and on the book spine were the words, *"Only Believe"*. I awoke from that vision with a sense to go deep in the word of God, only believing that which the spirit teaches out of the word.

Moses starts the Torah with a very significant introduction to his inspired story of creation. He lets us know Gods created mankind and put them in the Garden of Eden to rule the Earth, with purpose in mind. He uses the Hebrew word Elohim, indicating the plurality of the creator. Verse two introduces an often overlooked fact because traditionally, we have been taught and handed down translations which indicate the introduction of the

Holy Spirit; however the Hebrew Torah reads the words *"...Rûach Elohim"* which when translated means *"...Spirit Gods"* not as we know it to be "spirit of God". From the very beginning, Moses lets us know the spirits have Gods they worship. The spirits themselves are not gods rather they have "Gods".

Time travel back and I see the path walked getting thus far and then it becomes apparent it's always been the invisible one at work. As though living out a script, it appears this life has always been girded and guided by the Ghost who is holy, even when he was unknown to him, he provided in excess early on, not as a gift but as a test and waits ten years to tell you he was testing you and he will yet give what devils offered to lure you off him, which offer was botched in its infantile offering. I just cannot thank the high priest enough for his steadfastness. He was *"made perfect through the things he suffered"*. This was the fathers will, "that the author of our salvation be made perfect through his suffering" and once made perfect, he was appointed as heaven's high priest in the command of Melchizedek. The potency of this word just won't leave you alone. If you obey it long enough, you come under its power as it spells in the word. We are preserved by the Power of God and through the order which says, "Let all the Angels of God worship Him..." This command, all ghosts/spirits in heaven, on earth and under the earth must obey, practice the word of God. The world is our laboratory; the Bible, the theory. Let the word of Christ dwell in you richly and see you become more than a man, the angels will worship the man in Christ for Jesus is the head and we are his body, more so with the order of Melchizedek which says in Hebrews 1:6, "Let all the angels of God worship Him." We are gods, not over our fellow men but gods over all angels for the word of Melchizedek was spoken as a command to angels and not men.

A "god" is one whom all spirits must obey, not necessarily because they want to but because the very word which formed them is God and we have been born of God, by the word of God which lives and abides forever. So if you are in Christ, never forget who you are. This isn't just a believer's authority, no; this is who we are in Christ. The order of Melchizedek is all that we need know and understand and just as Jesus is a priest after the order of Melchizedek, we also have become priests after the order of Melchizedek for he is the head and we, his body, which order says, "Let all the angels of God worship Him..." We have been elevated as heirs of God and technically been made Gods over all spirits, more so with Psalm 82:6 saying, *"I have said, you are gods, and all of you are children of the Most-high God, but you shall die like ordinary men..."* letting us know that even right now in the flesh, we are gods, but we shall die like mere men, hence the reason why the believer dies just like every other man in the flesh. We are gods, not over our fellow men but gods over the angels, for the word of Melchizedek was spoken as a command to the angels and not to men. (Hebrews 1:6) When you are conscious of God in you as you speak, it will always be God speaking in and through you and the spirits must obey you. The earth is spirit infested; they are everywhere and they are not gods even though men worship them as gods. They are slaves to the Gods and that's just what they are, ministering spirits sent to earth from heaven to serve those amongst men deserving of God-ship, and for as many men you can see, there are much more spirits walking in and with those men whom you see.

"We proclaim to you what we have seen and heard, so that you also may have fellowship with us. And our fellowship is with the Father and with his Son, Jesus Christ." (1 John 1:3)

There are those who believe that the words *"ye are gods..."* as written in the books have little or no meaning to our present day living on earth. Jesus said, *"If he called them gods, unto whom the word of God came, and the scriptures cannot be broken"* who then are we to disbelieve his word? This is due to ignorance of God's word and comes not from the Lord, for they, in their callous heart hope to god over their fellow men, not reckoning with scripture that someone once said to God, *"What is man that you are mindful over him, or the son of man that you care about, you made him a little lower than angels for the suffering of death and crowned him with glory and honor..."* thus indicating even the angels wonder why man should be made to rule over them though man was initially created in a lower form of self. I say to you today, *"You are gods..."* Gods over the angels and not men. *"Do not rejoice that the angels are subject to you; rather rejoice that your names are written in heaven."* - *Jesus*

On earth and in heaven, only angels obey priests in the order of Melchizedek. Want to command angels? Study and learn more on the order of Melchizedek, its importance and why you should believe God's word. *"Are (angels) they not ministering spirits, sent forth to minister unto the heirs which shall inherit Salvation?* (Hebrews 1:14) "A priest after the order of Melchizedek," that's the man whom angels obey, not because the priest is anything of himself, no, but the one in whose command the priest is. That is how respected on one hand and feared on the other, Melchizedek is among the spirits. May the Gods grant you the grace to recognize your helper of destiny when they show up, they may not exactly be what you expect, but your destiny seed lies in them, and you are breeding ground for it to grow and deliver to you all your desires. Open your eyes that you may see the Spiritual is an art which takes a lifetime to study and observe and master.

The word of God is the book which opens you to the unseen, what separates us is what the teacher chooses to show you, but most importantly, who teaches you? Mine is the ghost, mine is the teacher from heaven. We are gods over the angels, this was the reason the earth was made in the first place, to test men and prove those deserving of ruler ship over all things created, both visible and invisible. This delusion of earthly existence serves as an obstacle course to determining who you really are, "I have said; ye are gods." The spirits refer to we who believe as priests; priests after the order of Melchizedek.

A priest is one called to divine service by God and is the appointed teacher of deep truths, more so when these include esoteric doctrines. By nature, he is native to the sacred dimension of life, which is the realm of the divine, and as such ought to conduct himself in a manner worthy of the command of Melchizedek, for he is anointed with knowledge in the mysteries of sacred profundity and divine power, and thus becomes the custodian of these secrets, he is expected to learn and understand them and in turn to entrust this esoteric knowledge to reliable men who are able to teach others. All servant spirits recognize the authority of the priests of the Most-high God; they recognize their word is law. We are priests of the Most-high God; I mean we are actual priests in the spirit realm, priests over all creation. For a long time we have misconstrued and misunderstood the meaning of the word priests, and this is because we view it from an earthly perspective, but we are not of this world, and should view ourselves from God's perspective because that is how he sees us, and that is how the devils see us, quite frankly, the devils would rather we remain ignorant of this truth, for they tremble at the thought of its being understood. *"Except a kernel of wheat falls into the ground and dies, it abides alone, but if it dies, it brings forth many more seeds..." - Jesus*

I died years ago and I will yet die again while I live, that I might be raised up an immortal God, in the fullness of all that is God in Jesus. In Glory, in strength, in wisdom, in power, incorruptible and eternally immortal will Elohim raise us up at the voice of Jesus, in that day we shall hear his voice, and when I say *we*, I mean our decomposed bodies, which have become dust shall once again gather together, from the nations where they have dispersed, each particle will come together and rise up to meet us and we will be reunited with our bodies we once left years ago while we yet lived in the flesh as we now do. The moment we get saved, his righteousness becomes our righteousness, all that Jesus has becomes ours, all that the Father has becomes ours, but the world's perception of "good" and "sinner" is flawed for they see us as they see themselves, not recognizing our status in Christ, for outwardly we all look the same, but inwardly we are being renewed day by day. Inwardly, we are Gods.

Many a time, in our walk with Christ we forget salvation is only the first step, we forget that Christ crucified is just a means to an end and not the end in itself, we forget the resurrection is just a part in the eternal story. We don't know Jesus is presently a high priest in heaven, so we talk about resurrection power as though it is the final end, not reckoning that Jesus today is a priest on the basis of the power of an endless life, the very same life in us, just as it is written, not on the basis of the resurrection power. However it is given to us through the spirit that we might understand the deep things of God. Many are called, few are chosen!

I believe it don't matter the opinion of men, what God says and thinks toward us is priority and of utmost importance. Blasphemy is a matter of Gods perspective, not mans, for man walks in darkness, barely able to see in the dark, and if the blind lead the blind, they both fall into a ditch, we walk in the light through the darkness enveloping the world, we are the light of the world and will not walk in darkness. Outside of all that we see with our eyes exists a world waiting to be discovered, and this is only possible by faith and faith in Jesus alone, *"No one pours new wine in old wine bottles, else the bottle will burst and the wine wasted, rather you pour new wine in new wine bottles and both are preserved..." - Jesus*

Bottom line is this, there are certain folks who just cannot receive a rhema word from God, just because it is new wine and they are old bottles. It was hard for Jesus to get his message across to the Pharisees because the message wasn't for them. It is the same story today; it is hard to get old bottles to hold the rhema word for the now, as it goes against all they ever thought was true, so the word will be given to a younger generation and this makes us the future.

If Christ be in you, you are the temple of God and God lives in you. When you allow God to be your mind, you and God are one, thus, you are God. Paul says, "He that is joined to the Lord is one spirit with the Lord..." This world we live in is an illusion. It is modeled after the parallel universe of heaven where God lives, but most live here as though this were the real world, not taking cognizance of the fact that if it were real, we would not be dying and exiting the world to the real place we emanated from. It appears Elohim is the grand Illusionist for having pushed us back to the world to till its soil; he set eternity in our hearts and gave us his word that we may live by the mirror it is, charting our course through life and beyond. Jesus said, *"...out of the abundance of the heart the mouth speaks..."* When you hear a teacher of God's word speak, know he brings forth his words out of his treasure chest within and the quality of his word depends on his depth of knowledge and insight spiritually.

Today, anyone picks up the book and say they been called but first of all, to be truly called isn't a jolly ride unless of course your purpose is less significant and as a result of less concern to the evil spirits that abound the earth we live in. Like Jonah, you may run in opposition to the call but God knows just how to get your attention. That's why I pity many who out of greed pick up the book and are ill prepared. Paul says he was compelled to preach, not necessarily because he wanted to rather as a duty entrusted to him. It's the same story today. Let your motive be right; if you do it willingly, you have a reward, if compelled then you are only discharging a trust. Whichever way, the word will be preached.

Here's a piece of advice. If you ever nursed the thought of seeing the future before it happens or knowing about past events which occurred in your absence, or knowing a person's thoughts while his words mean another, or speaking to the elements (e.g. fire) and it obeys you, or you just want to live supernatural, knowing events taking place in the realm of spirit in real-time, then look no further, this book is for you. The Word of God has it all. I am a Witness, but most of all, as you grow, let the love of God be your reason, for God's love only comes to us as we receive him, not before, and finally you must be willing to give him your mind that he may give you his own, for we have the mind of Christ and the spirit from God that we may know and understand the things freely given to us by God. My soul evolves into God while my body grows older. This is what Paul meant when he said, *"Though outwardly we are wasting away, yet inwardly we are being renewed day by day...But we all, with open face beholding as in a glass the glory of the Lord, are changed into the same image from glory to glory by the spirit of the Lord..."* (Spirit Revelation Evolves the Soul).

However hard we deny it, facts appear Christianity is more mystical and esoteric than it is religious and the earlier we embrace the deep truth of God's word, the better we are for it; else we keep binding and casting devils at war when in actual fact they should revere us either out of fear or willful submission. A man dies and rises from the dead and ascends to heaven, yet we call that religion? Those who believed on him went around doing the very same things he did while alive and yet we call that religion? Those who also believe on the stories written by those who saw that man also go about today doing the very same things the pioneer did and yet we dare call it religion. I choose the path of God's truth, no more religion, just pure spirituality in the Holy Ghost, enforcing the word, you may remain religious and keep fighting devils and the choice is yours.

There's a very thin line between being religious and being conscious of the invisible presence. These two, though closely linked and mistaken as alike, are not one and the same, while religion makes you "pious" with an appearance of Godliness, a conscious awareness in the soul raises perception and opens the eyes of the understanding to the invisible, even the mind's eye, so you certainly have no choice but to live by faith, even while others see you the same, for religious spirits do make war against the conscious soul awakened in Christ and as I discover myself, I realize I tend to dislike religion more and more. Religion is man's way of reaching out to God and it is an evil for it places on one the very chains of slavery which Christ has made us free of. To follow Christ is to walk the path of the initiate.

It is a path of esoteric doctrines and deep spiritual awareness. It is with disdain I see the many who say they are men of God, men whose god is their belly and who lack the basic knowledge of the spiritual elements of the doctrine of Christ. To follow Christ is to be drawn into a story that is nearly too good to be true but that is why it is the good news, and for two thousand years, the Jesus story remains the same, having the same foundation of Christ crucified and yet evolving in the entirety of its truth.

To follow Christ is to see angels and demons, fight against the forces who live to detract you, recognize the agents in human form, live with the eye of the mind and not judge by what you see with two eyes nor what you hear with two ears, rather by what you see and hear with the eye of your mind, which eye is your understanding of God's word. To follow Christ is a call to be God. A call to be God over the angels and demons; to follow Christ is to be led by the ghost from heaven. To follow Christ is many things too wonderful for words to explain. Religion does not know this. This life of the word is Spiritual, wake up to it. Fellowship with God comes through knowledge gained by the lights and perfections of God's word, never forget, once called, and always called. Once gifted, always gifted. *"For God's gifts and his call are irrevocable..."* (Romans 11:29) It is what you do with the gift and the call that matters, for me, it is my job to bring you in fellowship with the Mystery, which mystery is, Christ in you, and the hope of Glory. We do not fellowship with a God we barely know, rather our fellowship is with the father and his Son, Jesus Christ, the high priest of heaven, in the order and command of Melchizedek, the priest of God, whose command says, "let all the angels of God worship Him..." (Hebrews 1:6)

Chapter Seven

Musings Of A God

"A tree set on a hill cannot be hidden, no one lights a candle and puts it under a bed, it is set on a stand so it gives light to everyone coming in.." – Jesus

Voices

Voices from another realm, speaking words not taught of men, the spirit doth bid come, and come, the bride say. Halfway, they meet in union, for words yet to speak, words whose time doth wait, words bound in liberty, with silver and gold that never fade.

Voices from the dust of the earth, the departed souls of men do speak, in twain manners, cries are heard, even so laughing and praises. For here, the dead are undead, and happen upon the hidden truth that life doth exist beyond skin, with pain real as in flesh, with thirst to quench, with hunger to fill, with desire to live as flesh again, for here doth eternity unfold and reveal itself, the point of no return, right across the Rubicon.

Voices from hell's prisons, the watchers from above doth cry beneath, in vanity paying the price of lust, for having beheld the daughters of men in burning lust did we cry one to another, "Come, that we may be progenitors of a race". A race not created of Gods, a race whose primal origin is a, these hath Gods not spared, for in eternal chains they dwell, in the darkness of hell's prisons, never to see the light of day, and never to see their own race again until judgment doth come on its own day.

Voices from earth's unseen realm, the children of the watchers doth cry, "Giants we are, men and women of renown are we, not by our making, but demi-god's we are, fathered by angels, mothered by humans, with appetites inhuman, craving the taste of flesh, devoured man and beast alike did we, till the earth doth to Gods cry, for blood shed on it. Thus came our judgment, for Noah's floods did drown, demi-gods we were, but in flesh only, roam the earth do we, to avenge our fathers in hell's prisons, roam the earth do we, to oppress mankind, roam the earth do we, in hatred of the Gods. Evil spirits are we, male and female, for bodies drowned, have we none.

Reflections

For over 2000 years, the Jesus story remains the same and as the world evolves, the word also evolves. It remains on the firm foundation yet, the fellowship of the mystery gets thicker in its light, that Elohim did send the Son in human flesh who died, rose from the dead, ascended to heaven and is seated at the right hand of the Majesty. For over 2000 years, Jesus has been a high priest in heaven, not in the order of "Jesus"; rather He is a high priest in the order of Melchizedek, who is God's own priest forever, exactly as the books state it.

God will not have you go through all the tests and trials only to keep you down. He refines us in trials and afflictions that we may come out better than fine gold and once tested, he sends us into the world to give that which he put in us, that we may be a blessing to our generation. Selah.

Let the Lord gently lead you quietly. *"The first shall be last, and the last shall be first.* *"To whom much is given, much more is expected."* The Lord made it so easy; all you have to do is believe. The best part of our lives lies ahead of us, not behind. They live forever, Jehovah the King and Melchizedek the Priest. We know Jehovah the King and Melchizedek the Priest both make the Godhead and both created the world together through the Word and that's why one said to the other, "Let us make man in "our" image and later in "our" likeness. We have the fullness of the mystery and we know the hidden knowledge in the word of God. It's our portion, it's our responsibility, it's our God given mandate and we will spread it the world over. And for those who say, "My pastor didn't say so," I bet your pastor says, "Jesus is Melchizedek or Melchizedek is the Holy Spirit or an angel." Excuse me; you need milk, not strong meat. We know knowledge puffs up, but love edifies. Let us walk in love and bring Glory to the name above all names.

We are simply believers and priests in the command of Melchizedek. *"From now on, let no man trouble me, for I bear in my body, the marks of the Lord Jesus Christ. From the days of John the Baptist till now, the kingdom of God suffereth violence, and the violent take it by force..."* The church is placed beyond resurrection power; we talk the power that administers Gods word, the power that's always ruled next to the Most-high God, the King. The power of Melchizedek, the priest; The power of the order of Melchizedek, who is Gods priest forever in the heavens, the command regarding the Lord Jesus; choose this l of God, for with it, you attain immortality while you yet live in this body of flesh. Believe in your heart Jesus is Lord, say God raised him from the dead, and you have this life.

Sometimes we quote Jesus out of context, for example, he said, *"What God has joined together, let no man put asunder."* And we think all marriages were joined by the Lord because a minister officiated at the wedding. We need to understand the difference, what God has joined together is not the same as what man has joined together in the presence of God. There's a difference in the two and most of what we have today is what men (Pastors) have joined together in the presence of God. My advice to any, seek that which God joined together of his own will not that which you chose and men joined together before God. Who knows, the devils also join together. A classic example of what God joined together is the story of Joseph and Mary in the Bible. At least God spoke to them both prior to the union though they were espoused to each other.

With God's will, he desires more than the salvation of a man's soul, He further desires men grow to accurate knowledge of the truth. Don't stop here, keep moving. God is to you, who and what you perceive of him. To the crooked, God is crooked, to the plain, God is plain, to the wicked, God is wicked, and to the good, God is good. What you think of God is who God is to you. I really do not know what love is but if it's anything to go by, I would say, to know God is to know love. For God is love. Whoever controls the mind controls the man. This doesn't stem from a human perspective, it stems from the willful perspective of the forces of good and evil. Whoever gains the mind, wins the man and what happens to man when grace is over? Destruction, death plagues, wars, etc. in unprecedented levels! I sometimes wonder why men are quick to blame the devil for every plague of death. Revelation tells us, even with the plagues of death poured on the Earth by the angels of God, men would still harden their hearts and not turn to him...

Life's reality itself is a dream, and one day, you will wake up from it and ask what the real world is like? If indeed this life is a dream? Read the Holy Book and find out. The Holy Bible is The Mirror Book. It shows you truth you cannot ever perceive with your mind, nor see with your eyes, nor hear with your ears. It shows you the mind of the Godhead and the will of the father. Jesus revealed a God who seemed distinct from the God of the Old Testament, that's why the Jews of his day murdered him. The God Jesus revealed and the God of the Old Testament is one and the same Godhead, not one and the same person as expressed in words, one speaks judgment, the other speaks grace, one is God, the other is the Most-high God. Imagine the wrath and judgment of the Most-high God when the grace of God is over! The sayings of God are not secret in themselves; it is the interpretation of the sayings that are secret. This is the mystery, the proper interpretation of God's word. We value the high call of the invisible God, and we value the presence of the invisible spirits who reside with us and the greater spirit in us. It is an aberration of r to think the Godhead lives in temples made by human hands. We are priests, not man-made, but God-made priests in the spiritual order of Melchizedek and the spirit of the living God lives inside of us; we are his temple.

Ours is a journey to the ether world, a place where reality exists and earth is exposed as a hologram. Though we live in the world, we are not of the world, resounding truth it is, caught in the balance of living between two worlds, the earth's two realms appear, the visible we live in, wrapped in the invisible, for in him we live and move and have our being, our song is hidden from the many for he thought it fit only for Kings and Priests, concealed and veiled invisible, the truth stares in the face, yet remains unseen, the ghost is present, yet not perceived, for the music sings only to those he calls to dance. Much have we to say but you are dull of hearing, for though by now you ought to be teachers, you have need again to be taught the basics of the oracle of the Gods, Jehovah and Melchizedek, whose oracle is Jesus, the high priest of heaven, and when the time is right, just when the student is ready, the teacher will appear, for in the sands of time we are the future, then my soul will find you.

Salvation is only found in Jesus. The Jesus we know is not the baby Jesus born in the manger, yes he once was, and he once walked the earth in human skin. However, the Jesus we know is the present high priest in heaven, a priest after the order and command of Melchizedek, the priest of the Most-high God. The Jesus we know is the Jesus worshipped by all spirits, the very same Jesus by whom all spirits also are to worship us who believe in him, for he is the head, and we are his body. This is the command of Melchizedek is, "Let all the angels of God worship Him..."

It is amazing knowing you serve a God who cares so much about you, he tells you the future and only believes you believe him, for it's his only way of fulfilling his promises in our lives. May we have faith and patience to know his will for our lives, faith is a living force. What counts is what you do with it. For the things we see with our eyes are temporary, but the invisible we do not see is eternal, so we focus, not on the things we see with our eyes, rather, we focus on the invisible we cannot see, but believe. Follow those who through faith and patience obtained the promise... (Hebrews 6)

God's end plan for humanity is turning men into Gods. So we do not look and focus our minds on what is seen, rather we focus on what is unseen, for what is seen, everything that is seen is temporal, including our bodies, but what we do not see and yet we believe, is eternal. Man is not a rational being, else how do we explain we believe in a God whom we do not see, except by "faith"?

Always remember, just like a movie script, only this is real, we are never alone, every man, male or female, is accompanied by an invisible spirit. This is true, whether or not you believe it. This is truth we hardly hear in the church buildings. This is exactly what Jesus meant when he said of the spirit, *"he will be with you and in you forever."* much more the number of angels present. This is the meat the church needs for spiritual maturity and growth, not so much talk about money, turning God's house to business centers. *"To whom you yield yourselves slaves to obey, his servants you are, whether of sin which leads to death, or obedience which leads to life everlasting..."* The choice is yours. *"The man without the spirit cannot accept the words that come from the Spirit of God, for they are foolishness to him, neither can he understand them, for they are spiritually understood"* We know in part and we speak forth (about what we know) in part. There comes a time when the rivers can no longer hold and they burst forth, when the time comes, swim with the tide, not against it, and may let the Lord gently lead you quietly, Amen.

The coming days will separate those who believe there is God, from those who know their God. The demons also believe there is God, and they tremble, stand your ground and give no place to the enemy of your soul. Buckle up, no excuses. You never know what you're capable of being until you try to be. Reality is what we perceive it to be not necessarily what it is. It is the norms we were raised with, traditions handed down to us, and these things basically form the basis for what we perceive as existing reality. What God's word does to the relative observer who not only believes, but observes to do, is this; it reshapes reality. Once you start to perceive the observable effects of God's word, you start to see the very things the eyes do not perceive, you live from the higher perspective, and unfortunately, you will be misunderstood by many. Preachers are comfortable with the six foundational doctrines as listed in Hebrews 6, forgetting the author says, *"Therefore let us move toward maturity, NOT LAYING AGAIN the foundation of repentance from dead works, and of faith toward God, the doctrine of baptism, the laying on of hands, the resurrection of the dead and eternal judgment..."* The apostle speaks of resurrection as a foundation doctrine, whether the power raising the dead or the dead raised with power, this he says is milk. Demand more from your teachers. As bishops over your souls, they are responsible to feed you and ensure growth is experienced. For this they shall account for...! The earlier you begin to understand the truth the better, for truth revealed ceases to be a mystery. And just because you don't hear it from your "pastor" doesn't make it wrong, he just might not know.

"The angel of the Lord encamps all around those who fear him and delivers them." (Psalm 34:7)

Normally, we read the above and normally we do not perceive the reality of its words. The truth David tried to tell us above is this; there is an invisible angel who goes everywhere with you and never leaves your side, his job is to protect you and deliver you from every form of evil. It is your job to believe this by faith and whether or not you do is up to you. The ruler of peace is the ruler of righteousness, and as the name implies, Melchizedek is the ruler of peace and of righteousness, just as Jesus is our peace and our righteousness, and yet Jesus is a priest forever after the order of Melchizedek in heaven. The spiritual civil war we find ourselves in was initially between the spirits alone, but man got involved when one of their own in the person of Jesus, ascended to the realm of spirits, took over the position of another God, and continues dishing out war instructions, now not just to spirit, but also to men. My advice; find your place in this war, that you might not become casualty, which casualty is first spiritual, then physical. Man got directly involved in it after the resurrection, before the resurrection, the war had always been there, but Jesus had to die for man to be redeemed and exalted. Before Jesus came, we could not rebuke devils and they obey us but after his resurrection, we here on earth became directly involved, not before. The Bible is replete with revelations of diverse and different levels, all done by the same spirit and Lord.

Man was placed in Eden after his creation for a purpose. He was to rule the earth from Eden and he was to rule the earth as a god who lives in Eden, but rules over the affairs of earth which would be inhabited by animals. This was God's original plan. After the fall, man is himself driven into the world he was to rule as a god, only this time he is the only intelligent being on the planet he was to rule and this is a direct result of his being made in image and likeness unto Elohim. Careful study reveals Adam was meant to rule the earth from the Garden of Eden; it was after his fall that man was driven out of the Garden to till the earth he was taken from. Ezekiel reveals, Lucifer once was domiciled in the Garden of Eden, "Thou hast been in Eden, the Garden of God..." apparently he was viceroy over the earth and all that was on the earth long before Adam was created. Upon his fall, he was thrown to the earth. Satan was never in hell.

The Dead Shall Rise Again

What is sown is not what will be, what is sown in the ground comes out differently. When a seed is sown, perhaps maize, it is sown as a seed, but when it is time to germinate, it comes out differently and finally appears in full stalks of corn, even so with the resurrection of the dead, our bodies are sown in a dishonored state into the ground (1 Cor. 15), but at the end of days, at the sound of Jesus, by the order of Melchizedek, we who believe shall be raised up immortal. In immortality, we shall reign over all spirits who presently terrorize many amongst us and we will "revenge all disobedience when our obedience is complete..." (2 Cor.10:10)

We shall be changed into the very likeness of Elohim; we shall become Gods, both male and female. "Now are we the sons of God, but it does not yet appear what we shall be, but we know that when he appears, we shall be like him, for we shall see him as he is..." Presently, in spirit, we are Gods, but we do not look like it outwardly, as we got saved, we retained human bodies, so we share the likeness of God in spirit and the likeness of men in flesh, (isn't it wonderful), the world sees us as they see themselves, but when Jesus comes, we shall be raised up with a different body. 1 Cor. 15 says, "As there is a natural body, there is also a spiritual body..." In Chapter 15 of his first Epistle to the Corinthians, Apostle Paul says, *As there is a natural body, there is also a spiritual body..."* This is so true, for spirits do have bodies, though as spirits, they are not perceived by the senses of men but in the realm they have primal origin, a spirit cannot walk through a wall, just as God sits on his throne and the chair holds him up. He doesn't fall through the throne, no, it is as solid as he is solidly seated on it. Open your eyes and see, transformation takes place as our eyes are enlightened.

Jesus said, "I hold the keys of hell and death..." You want know who he took the keys from? Look to the scriptures, whose job did he take over when he ascended to heaven? He became the present high priest in the order of whom? Melchizedek! At the right hand of the Father, Jesus said, "I hold the keys of hell..." He never said he took it from the devil. I wonder where men got that notion from that Jesus took the keys of hell from the devil.

Spell God's Word

Growing up, we were all taught to spell words, and the words we spelled gave meaning to what we gave them, spell and spelling is the putting together of alphabets to create meaning and eventually words are what we say they are, then comes pronunciation, we learn to Spell words in speech. In the beginning, Elohim spelled words in the sentence, "Let there be light," and there was light, let's learn to spell God's word over our lives, and see it manifest, it's the first process in creating and recreating our world... Bring yourself under the power of God and Spell his word over your life through obedience to his word, this is the only way to come under the Spell of God's word, when I say obedience to his word, it's not just doing good to others, it's beyond that, at this level, you need to rule over the spirits, and have them subject to you. The only way to achieve that is by coming under the Spell and command of God's word which says, "Let all the angels of God worship him (Jesus)" believing the order of Melchizedek says all Spirits should worship Jesus, and "we are complete in Christ who is the head of all principalities and power..." A believer's authority is in the message he's been given to speak, speak the words given to you, you serve a purpose and your words are pillars to hold others up, you never know who needs it; surely it is in great need out there. Remember: Peter got out of the boat and walked toward Jesus and was doing fine until he doubted, Then he started sinking. Jesus' reply: "You of little faith. Why did you doubt?" Friends, what miracles are your doubts keeping you from performing?

Truth is our perception of "Christianity" is faulty. The believer is NOT the pious image we have been made to believe we ought to be, the transforming power of God's word doesn't make us naive, "the righteous is bold as a lion..." The truth of God's word is far from any and most of what we have been taught. "We did not follow cleverly devised myths, but were eyewitnesses of his glory..." Peter uses the word MYTHS, because that's what the full picture of the Jesus story would look like. When you start to understand the weight the "order of Melchizedek" carries, you start to walk in the knowledge of the authority of the Godhead. Hebrews 1:6 says, "When he brought in the firstborn, he said, LET ALL THE ANGELS OF GOD WORSHIP HIM..." It starts here and now, a heavenly proclamation, spiritual and cosmic in nature, an invisible event which takes place at the ghosts' party, declared in the unseen realm and yet its effects reach into the seen realm we live. Here we see why at the mention of the name of Jesus, every knee should bow, of in heaven, of on earth and under the earth. This is the command of Melchizedek, heaven's priest. God's word is TRUTH and we remain the GHOST'S APPRENTICE while we yet live in the flesh. At times, I ponder on what folks mean when they say people should see God in the Christian because men looked at Jesus and saw a rebel and a blasphemer worthy of death. How then should anyone today expect to see God in the Christian? Considering the truth Jesus said, "If they persecuted me, they will also persecute you." Truth be told, men can never see God in the Christian unless of course they themselves have the light of truth and look beyond the flaws of imperfection to the perfect state of the human spirit.

You have to die as a seed that you may live as a tree. This is likened to what Jesus meant when he said, "Except a grain of wheat falls into the ground and dies, it abides alone..." Be ready to give up the things which so easily set you back that you may bear more fruit to the praise and glory of God, creating in others that which God created in you. When Jesus spoke the above, he referred to himself as the seed, his death and resurrection brought forth many just like him, only this time, we don't need to die to reproduce, while we live we bring forth our kind, conceiving them with the word and giving birth to others just like us. It is the same motion of reproduction as set by Elohim, we bring forth after our kind. Spirit begets spirit, flesh begets flesh, save a life today and give birth, get a man born again by leading him to Christ. The persecution we face is stirred up by the spirits who don't want the truth revealed. So if you ever find a Preacher being persecuted, do not judge, for it could just be a lie to get him killed for speaking the truth of God's word just as Jesus was. And we will surpass the persecution that comes with the knowledge of the truth.

Sometimes, to get your attention, God gets you in a corner where you have little choice but to choose his offer. This doesn't apply to all, it just means you're chosen and no longer your own, so rather than fight his will, embrace it and save yourself the pain. We have the capacity to become slaves to our faith, which is the believer's forte. We have the capacity to believe and that is why the gospel of Jesus has come to stay. There are some things prayers will not do for you and some things that prayers cannot alter nor change. In such times, what you need is just one word from God. Just one word from God, said from your lips puts paid on that situation. You need understanding. Rebuke Satan and he will flee from you. At times, I wonder on the simpleton man is and how far removed from his thoughts his true nature, a specie born with Amnesia, man in his highest material state is boastful and proud, and that's where man is foolish.

For if reason abode with him, he would consider his frail state and seek that which has eternal value. For in our truest form, we did bring nothing into the world other than the soul we are, which soul in itself is spirit in nature, so then how and why few ponder on the true meaning of life's existence, if after all said and done, the body which made us proud goes back to dust, and each return to the true eternal state which man really us, spirit. Why then are men so foolish not to ponder on the truth of life, for surely it's not about wealth accumulation, which wealth in itself is good. Why don't we seek that with eternal value, that which brings to mind while in this body, knowledge of our true state before we were sent to the earth, to be born mortal.

Surely, we all existed before coming to this world to be tested to glory, seek the knowledge that is you, seek the light of God's word, accepting Jesus is only the first step and is just enough to get you through the judgment, but possessing the truth of who you are and were before being sent here to be tested qualifies you for a prize, therefore run that you may win.

The devil, Lucifer, and his cohorts have been so inured with lies that even when they speak the truth, it is thought to be a lie. *"When he speaketh a lie, he speaketh on his own (it comes natural to him for it is his nature), for he is a liar and the father of all lies."* In Philippi, the slave girl who followed Paul and Silas for three days kept telling the men, "these men are servants of the Most-high God," she spoke the truth but it was a demon speaking through her, this happened until Paul was grieved in his spirit on the third day and called out the demon from within her.

We were raised up with Christ, made to sit at the right hand of the Majesty on high and when he was presented before the heavenly world, we were in Him when the command was issued to all spirits saying, "Let all the angels of God worship Him." As they worship the head, they worship the body. My God lives within me by his spirit. I take him everywhere I go; I am one with him, he lives within, I live without. We are one; one body, one soul, one mind, one word, and one God. I love the gospel for it gives us the opportunity to lead two lives in two worlds. One where we appear as the carpenter and yet a son of the Most-high, or as fishermen and yet sons of a great God, or you could choose to be the tax collector and still be a foundational block in the kingdom, or the woman who's had five husbands and yet be accepted in the beloved or the teacher of the law who sought wisdom from the master at night. All these knew who they were and became but the world of men saw them from the frail perspective of society's warped vision. Ordinary they appeared, but gods they were and became. In any war, always choose the winning side. Men we appear, but Gods we are.

If we could hear the voices of the dead, we would ponder on our present lives and make amends where necessary. Though the dead speak only in one of two tones, the former being a resounding song of joy for having left this miserable plane of existence while the latter with tears of anguish of soul. The souls of the dead realize how weak they are, though once powerful upon the earth, in hell, they say to each other, "We have become weak as the rest, our worms, like us, do not die, have mercy on us O' Lord."

Plead they do, yet no respite from their suffering. These ones were once powerful on the earth, they oppressed all others, lived above law as politicians and lawgivers, they cared not for the oppressed of the land, nor the Lord who gave them breath, and their portion is with the wicked beneath the earth. Which would it be for you? The answer rests with you in the now, for hereafter, there only remains one of both choices. Consider the gamble well spent, but remember, the choice is yours. The earlier you attain self-consciousness of this one truth in God's word, the better for you who believe in Jesus. You are a god over all angels, cherubim and seraphim, over all powers here present on earth or in the unseen realm.

It is your responsibility to take charge of that which is yours and awaken the conscious mind of Christ in you. And to think they once thought we were crazy, we who believed Jesus became the high priest in heaven after the order of Melchizedek! Now they preach the same words they once condemned. Everything spiritual, all which is concealed and hidden will be revealed, so marvel not at the words we speak for they are words of life.

My thoughts wander, cast upon the word to which we are born of, what then is life here on earth? Certainly not being born, grow to youth, acquire wealth, grow old and die? Certainly not, for if that were it then of all creatures seen, man is the most miserable. No doubt portals are open, light and illumination beckon us forth to the heralding of a new dawn, a time when purpose and clarity are clearly seen, being understood in time's eternal flow. Eternity beams forth, for out of the darkness, we shine forth, commanded to appear at the word of the eternal God, for such a time as this we were called upon, a shove into destiny it is, and destiny we must embrace, for of immortality and spirit have we been born, called and chosen to manifest in these times with words not our own. A priest forever after the command of Melchizedek, the invisible priest of God, we make the fellowship of the mystery plain and still many think it's not needful for the now. The Apostle Paul says the same to the Ephesians in Chapter 3. We make plain the "FELLOWSHIP OF THE MYSTERY" to all men, that they may partake of the many spiritual blessings in the heavenly realm right here on earth, mastering the spirits while we yet live on earth. It is short minds, who would find it absurd that God is male and female, exactly in the same shape in which man exists, male and female, it is written and it is so. Nothing can change this.

In perilous times as we live in, we must sincerely ask the right questions. No doubt the world is headed to WW3 and the battle ground was chosen long before now. SYRIA, as we know it, is a ground wherein nations will gather to do battle. This is not a war as conventional warfare dictates, it is a war fought with proxies. Armies mobilize, the people remain blind to see it start, and thousands have fled the nation to give way for weapons test, enough room for ballistic exchange. We must pray, for the coming days will separate many and a chasm will appear. Pray especially for Jerusalem, for the time approaches, men are moved against men by the counterparts' unseen with each one, all depends where you stand and the ghost standing with you. Revelation unveils, and being vigilant we are victorious. A third temple shall stand, not as a sign of victory, but as the abomination that causes desolation, for Elohim does not live in temples made with human hands. And when this happens, *"Let him who is in the mountains flee..." (Matthew 24)* and gradually, the end approaches.

Amen

.

Conclusion

September 14, 2001, after a lengthy two weeks, the fast with prayers came to an end. At the time; he was a member of Christ Embassy Church aka Believers Loveworld, Inc. As darkness covered the earth, in visions of the night, there appeared an angel; the scene was set in ancient Jerusalem, from whence they moved to Rome. Apparently, the angel seemed a tour guide, while as he appeared to be the fifth man walking the line behind the angel as he explained to them all the events foregoing the collapse of Jerusalem and Rome. After a while the angel stops, turns and says, "*Later, read the book of Micah 2:8, also read Haggai 2:6-9*", to which we nodded in response. Further down the path, there appeared a footbridge which they crossed in sequence with the angel at the head of the line and he at the last, when suddenly, the man in front of him stops, turns and whispers, "*Let me tell you a secret, this will help you a lot, read 2 Corinthians 5:7.*" At this, he saw himself in his room, with the same clothes he fell asleep in and suddenly the night sky begins to wobble, a portal was opened with lightning coming from the east and west end of the portal, meeting in the middle of the opening and approaching towards the earth, right towards the steel grill of his window. Awestruck by the sight and without cognizance of a presence moving towards him, suddenly he is picked up and flung across the far room. Hitting the wall and looking up simultaneously, he sees the image of a man but could see through the image to the wall behind this image. The presence moves towards him again, raises him to the ceiling fan, at which he kept screaming and suddenly realized the fan couldn't hurt him. As though the creature read his thoughts, it flung him towards the window from whence he saw the lighting coming to the earth and began to squeeze him against the steel grill. He screams at the top of his voice, struggling with the creature, until he remembered and said, "*Jesus.*" At which name, the creature let go of him as though struck with the word. At this, he commands with a wave of his left hand, "*In the name of Jesus, get out of here.*" At whose command, the image moved out as fast as it came in and then he awoke. And since the demons wouldn't leave him alone, he dug his heels in and chose to fellowship with the mystery of God's word, now choosing to do the work entrusted to him by the Gods that through this he might *"have a readiness to revenge all disobedience, when his obedience will have been complete..."* in death.

THIS IS THE COMMAND OF MELCHIZEDEK

THIS IS THE FELLOWSHIP OF THE MYSTERY

Faith is to you what you perceive it to be as God is to you what you perceive him to be, yet one thing is certain, faith is faith, as God is God, unchanging in nature, ever constant, consistent and fully present even in the face of doubt..

THE COMMAND OF MELCHIZEDEK

CPSIA information can be obtained
at www.ICGtesting.com
Printed in the USA
LVOW08s1259050617
536975LV00001B/37/P